BIRDING CRANE RIVER: NEBRASKA'S PLATTE

GARY R. LINGLE
1994

Illustrated by William S. Whitney and Ernest V. Ochsner

HARRIER PUBLISHING
P.O. BOX 5352
GRAND ISLAND, NEBRASKA 68802-5352

Library of Congress Catalog Card Number: 94-76921

ISBN Number: 0-9641219-0-5

First Edition
6   5   4   3   2   1
Printed in the United States of America

Published and Distributed by
> Harrier Publishing
> P.O. Box 5352
> Grand Island, Nebraska 68802-5352

Maps (Inside backcover)
> Scott Purdy

Illustrations
> William S. Whitney
> Ernest V. Ochsner

Layout and Design
> Gary R. Lingle
> William S. Whitney

Cover Photography
> Sandhill Cranes on the Platte; John G. Sidle

To my son, Ryan,
with the hope that your enjoyment of Nature never wanes.

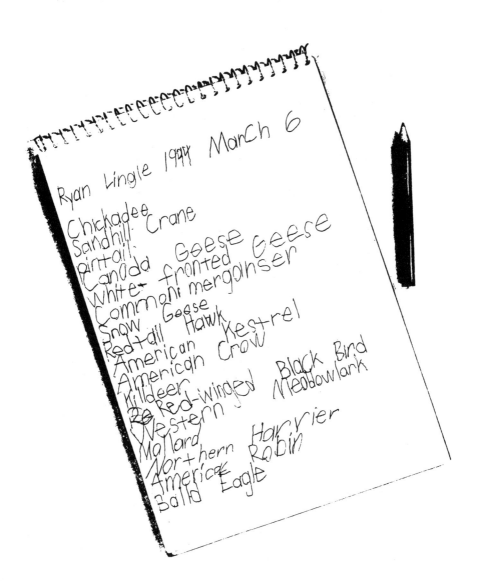

American Birding Association Code of Ethics

We, the Membership of the American Birding Association, believe that all birders have an obligation at all times to protect wildlife, the natural environment, and the rights of others. We therefore pledge ourselves to provide leadership in meeting this obligation by adhering to the following general guidelines of good birding behavior.

I. Birders must always act in ways that do not endanger the welfare of birds or other wildlife.

In keeping with this principle, we will

- Observe and photograph birds without knowingly disturbing them in any significant way.
- Avoid chasing or repeatedly flushing birds.
- Only sparingly use recordings and similar methods of attracting birds and not use these methods in heavily birded areas.
- Keep an appropriate distance from nests and nesting colonies so as not to disturb them or expose them to danger.
- Refrain from handling birds or eggs unless engaged in recognized research activities.

II. Birders must always act in ways that do not harm the natural environment.

In keeping with this principle, we will

- Stay on existing roads, trails, and pathways whenever possible to avoid trampling or otherwise disturbing fragile habitat.
- Leave all habitat as we found it.

III. Birders must always respect the rights of others.

In keeping with this principle, we will

- Respect the privacy and property of others by observing "No Trespassing" signs and by asking permission to enter private or posted lands.
- Observe all laws and the rules and regulations which govern public use of birding areas.
- Practice common courtesy in our contacts with others. For example, we will limit our requests for information, and we will make them at reasonable hours of the day.
- Always behave in a manner that will enhance the image of the birding community in the eyes of the public.

IV. Birders in groups should assume special responsibilities.

As group members, we will

- Take special care to alleviate the problems and disturbances that are multiplied when more people are present.
- Act in consideration of the group's interest, as well as our own.
- Support by our actions the responsibility of the group leader(s) for the conduct of the group.

As group leaders, we will

- Assume responsibility for the conduct of the group.
- Learn and inform the group of any special rules, regulations, or conduct applicable to the area or habitat being visited.
- Limit groups to a size that does not threaten the environment or the peace and tranquility of others.
- Teach others birding ethics by our words and example.

(Reprinted with permission from ABA).

Preface

I first came to Nebraska in the spring of 1978 but it wasn't until the following March that I experienced the magic of the crane migration along the Platte. It has become a much-anticipated annual event in my life ever since. Neither words nor film can capture the magic of witnessing a roosting flight of cranes with pink hues of dawn as a backdrop. With the increasing media attention given to the cranes and waterfowl each spring, crane-watching has become a major tourist attraction, pumping over $40 million into the central Platte River valley economy annually. The need for a guide to the area was apparent 20 years ago; now it is essential. I hope this guide will fulfill that need.

As is the case with any guide of this type, it is in constant need of revision and updating. The species list is based largely on my personal observations from 1978 to 1994 along with sightings published in the *Nebraska Bird Review* and reports made directly to me. I will assume responsibility for any omissions or errors. In order to place some measure on the chances of sighting a particular species, I subjectively placed an "Observability" code for each species ranging from 1 to 5 with 1 being almost certain to see and 5 being those species that are accidental to the area. No attempt was made to rank the relative abundance of a species on a month-by-month basis as other birding guides have endeavored to do.

I have highlighted only a few of the good birding areas found within each county. It is hoped that birders will use the enclosed maps and seek out their own "hotspots". Local water conditions will dictate which of the Rainwater Basin wetlands offer the best potential. During wet years, any of the basins marked on the maps will attract a variety of waterbirds. During dry years, only the larger basins or those that are filled by pumping groundwater by government agencies will contain enough water to attract any numbers of birds. The *Local Contacts* section of this guide will give you the telephone numbers and addresses of the appropriate organizations that can provide you with current information. The bird list should serve as a challenge to you to "tick" a new month for a species or perhaps add a new species to the list. I will be grateful to receive any comments you have about this guide or sighting records that may be used to update future editions.

The number of people who shared their observations with me is too long to list each of them; however, several names must be mentioned. Thomas Labedz, collections manager of the Nebraska State Museum, not only shared his own sightings, but provided pertinent records contained in the vertebrate collections of the museum and also critically reviewed this manuscript. Paul Bedell added to this effort as well, meticulously recording his sightings and sharing them with me. In particular, a number of members of the Nebraska Ornithologists' Union, Big Bend Audubon, and the Grand Island Chapter of Audubon shared their observations. Working with the Platte River Whooping Crane Trust enabled me to become very familiar with the avifauna of this region, having spent literally thousand's of hours studying birds as the staff ornithologist. Bill and Jan Whitney were a source of inspiration and I spent many hours discussing all sorts of topics related to the natural history of the area with them. Jan and John G. Sidle provided valuable editorial comments as well. My mother was a tireless source of encouragement. And I must not forget the excited observations of my son, Ryan, who was spotting cranes and eagles and owls by the time he was 3 years old. Perhaps that excitement of a child discovering the wonders of Nature inspired me the most. I hope this guide will assist you to experience the thrill of discovery as you explore a truly unique place.

Happy Birding!

Gary Lingle
6614 Whooping Crane Drive
Wood River, NE 68883

June 1994

TABLE OF CONTENTS

i.	Dedication	3
ii.	ABA Code of Ethics	4
iii.	Preface	5

I.	**Introduction**	**11**
	The Physical Setting	12
	Biogeography	12
	Geology	12
	Weather/Climate	14
	Habitat Changes	15
	Planning Your Trip	17
	Food/Lodging	17
	Pests	17

II.	**Birding Areas by County**	**19**
	Adams	23
	Buffalo	27
	Clay	31
	Hall	35
	Hamilton	41
	Kearney	45
	Phelps	49

III.	**Specialties of the Region**	**51**
	The Main Attractions	51
	Sandhill Crane	51
	Waterfowl	51
	Threatened and Endangered Species	56
	Bald Eagle	56
	Peregrine Falcon	58
	Whooping Crane	58
	Piping Plover and Least Tern	60
	Eskimo Curlew	61
	Other Species of High Interest	62
	Waders	62
	Raptors	62
	Shorebirds	66
	Greater Prairie-Chicken and Sharp-tailed Grouse	67
	Upland Sandpiper	68
	American Woodcock	70
	Franklin's Gull	71
	Burrowing Owl	72
	Red-headed Woodpecker	73
	Northern Flicker	73
	Willow Fycatcher and Bell's Vireo	75
	Eastern and Western Kingbird	75
	Cliff Swallow	76
	Black-billed Magpie	76
	Sedge Wren	76

TABLE OF CONTENTS

Eastern Bluebird	78
Loggerhead Shrike	80
Dickcissel	80
Grasshopper Sparrow	81
Harris' Sparrow	82
Bobolink	82
Eastern and Western Meadowlark	84
Yellow-headed Blackbird	85
Great-tailed Grackle	85
Northern Oriole	85
House Finch	86

IV.	**Birds of the Platte**	**87**
V.	**Local Contacts and Conservation Organizations**	**100**
VI.	**Additional Reading**	**107**
VII.	**Other Terrestrial Vertebrates**	**110**
	List of Amphibians and Reptiles	111
	List of Mammals	112
VIII.	**Sighting Report Form**	**114**
IX.	**Index**	**115**
X.	**Order Form**	**123**

List of Figures

1.	The Rainwater Basin	13
2.	Average Temperature at Grand Island, Nebraska	14
3.	Average Precipitation at Grand Island, Nebraska	15
4.	Map of Adams County	22
5.	Map of Buffalo County	26
6.	Map of Clay County	30
7.	Map of Hall County	34
8.	Map of Hamilton County	40
9.	Map of Kearney County	44
10.	Map of Phelps County	48
11.	Crane-watching Etiquette	52
12.	Sunrise/Sunset Table	54
13.	Chronology of Waterfowl Migration	55
14.	Mid-winter Bald Eagle Survey for Nebraska	58
15.	Fall Count of Whooping Cranes at Aransas, Texas	59
16.	Number of Species Observed by Month	99

TABLE OF CONTENTS

Illustrations

1. Northern Harrier over Marsh   20
2. Horned Lark- Taylor Ranch   32
3. Bobolink in Meadow   38
4. Regal Fritillary   42
5. Upland Sandpiper in Meadow   46
6. Sandhill Cranes   51
7. Bald Eagle Raids Basin   56-57
8. Piping Plover Nest   60
9. Great Horned Owl, Late Winter Nest- Platte Bluffs   63
10. Swainson's Hawks Over Ratzlaff Prairie- Spring Burn   65
11. Upland Sandpiper   69
12. Mid-day meal, Franklin's Gulls, Platte Bluffs   70-71
13. Red-headed Woodpecker & Bush Clover   74
14. Sedge Wren & Nest   77
15. Eastern Bluebird   79
16. Dickcissel   80
17. Grasshopper Sparrow   81
18. Bobolink   83
19. Western Meadowlark   84
20. Feather   86
21. Wet Meadow in July   99

INTRODUCTION

In the heart of the Central Flyway lies a broad, braided river - the Platte- and a region of scattered wetlands known collectively as the Rainwater Basin. It is here that the hourglass shaped flyway narrows, funneling millions of cranes, waterfowl, shorebirds, and other species from throughout the Western Hemisphere into the Platte River valley and Rainwater Basin. Few wildlife spectacles rival the spring migration of Sandhill Cranes through the Platte valley, and nowhere else in the world do cranes of any species congregate in the numbers that occur here in Nebraska. In late February, the cranes and huge flocks of waterfowl begin to arrive, their numbers building weekly until their departure by early April. Nearly 500,000 cranes and over 10 million ducks and geese stage here, building up vital fat reserves which will fuel them to their Arctic nesting grounds as far away as northern Canada, Alaska, and Siberia.

The allure of this concentration of birds is such that birding guru Roger Tory Peterson considers the area among his twelve favorite birding hotspots in North America, and well it should be. A visit to the Platte in March is a must for anyone with even a remote interest in birds or nature. The sights and sounds of a half million birds excites your senses and rejuvenates your spirit like nothing else can. Indeed the increasing popularity of this region as a destination among nature enthusiasts served as an impetus to produce this guide.

Certainly cranes and waterfowl are the most conspicuous feathered inhabitants of the area; however, they comprise less than 10% of the 300+ species found here. Six federally endangered/threatened species occur here as well. They are the Bald Eagle, Peregrine Falcon, Whooping Crane, Piping Plover, Eskimo Curlew, and Least Tern.

This guide will attempt to address the most often asked questions regarding birding in the area. I hope that it will motive you to explore this unique place and assist you in developing an appreciation of this area.

THE PHYSICAL SETTING

BIOGEOGRAPHY- Not only do the Platte River and adjacent Rainwater Basin lie in the "belt" of the Central Flyway's hourglass; they also fall in the heart of the Great Plains near the center of the North American continent. The Platte River valley provides a forested riparian highway connecting the coniferous forests of the Rocky Mountains to the eastern deciduous forests of the Missouri Valley. Consequently, this is a region of biological crossroads, where east meets west and north meets south. It is a zone of hybridization for a number of species and/or populations such as Rose-breasted x Black-headed Grosbeaks, Indigo x Lazuli Buntings, "Yellow-shafted" x "Red-shafted" Flickers, and "Baltimore" x "Bullock's" Orioles. Southern species like the Mississippi Kite and Northern Mockingbird are near their northern limit here while northern species such as the Northern Shrike and Pine Siskin are near their southern limit.

GEOLOGY/HYDROLOGY- Elevations in the region vary from about 2500 feet to 1700 feet above sea level. The Platte River dates back to about 100,000 years ago during an interglacial period following the Pleistocene. The Platte Valley is underlain by a Quaternary alluvium of clay, silt, sand, and gravel. Beneath this lies an interfingering bed of similar materials which form the porous and highly permeable Ogallala Formation. A huge underground reservoir known as the Ogallala Aquifer lies beneath much of the central plains and is found here. Alluvial bottomlands, river terraces, and gently rolling bluffs above the river escarpment comprise the dominant topographic features of

valley. The primary source of water in the river is snowpack in
the Rocky Mountains of Colorado and Wyoming. There are no
major tributaries feeding the central Platte. The general relief of
the river is about 7 feet per mile and it flows to the east. The
valley is broad and flat. The "Big Bend" reach of the Platte is an
80-mile stretch from Lexington to Grand Island.

The Rainwater Basin encompasses 4,200 square miles within 17
counties of southcentral Nebraska. It lies generally south of the
Platte River in the Loess Plains Region of Nebraska - flat to
gently rolling plains formed by deep deposits of wind-blown silt
loam soils. Surface drainage is poorly developed resulting in
numerous silt-lined depressions that do not intercept the
groundwater table. These depressions are fed exclusively from
surface water runoff; hence their designation as rainwater basins.

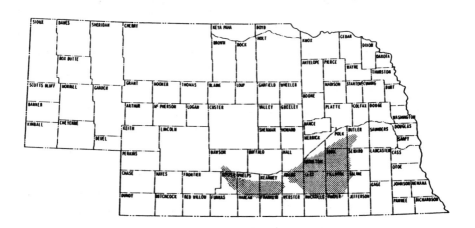

The Rainwater Basin

WEATHER/CLIMATE- Southcentral Nebraska has a
continental climate characterized by hot summers, frigid winters,
and irregular precipitation. Violent weather is an annual
occurrence and includes tornadoes, blizzards, hail, high winds, ice
storms, and thunderstorms often accompanied by intense
lightning. Extreme temperatures vary from -26°F to 117°F, with
wind chills often exceeding -50°F. In Grand Island, the average
annual high temperature is 62°F and the average annual low is

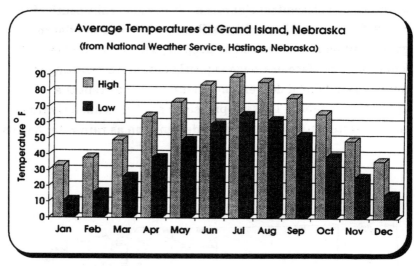

38°F. Wide temperature fluctuations can occur daily and it is not
uncommon for temperatures to exceed 60°F during winter.
January is the coldest month, averaging 23.7°F, and July is the
hottest, averaging 78°F. Average frost dates are May 1 and
October 8. Mean annual precipitation is 24.9", with an average of
30.3" of snowfall. Winds are moderately strong, averaging 11.8
mph annually, and generally occur from the south in summer and
northwest in winter. On two occasions in 1993, winds exceeded
100 mph, toppling large trees and damaging farmsteads and
utility lines. Travelers should be prepared for all kinds of
weather. Raingear, adequate boots, and warm clothing which can
be worn in layers are strongly recommended, especially for

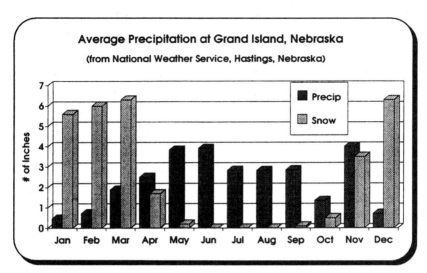

anyone coming to view cranes in March. The old cliché, "If you don't like the weather, wait a day (hour)," is certainly appropriate here.

HABITAT CHANGES- If you fly over central Nebraska, the Platte River appears as a winding thread of habitat in a sea of corn. Prior to settlement by Europeans, the landscape of southcentral Nebraska was dominated by tallgrass prairie. This landscape was shaped by the effects of large herbivores (bison, pronghorn, wapiti), weather, and fire which was often set by native Americans. In the last 150 years, the descendents of European settlers have molded the landscape to suit their needs. Gone are the vast herds of free roaming bison and immense flocks of Eskimo Curlews and Passenger Pigeons. Gone is the seemingly endless sea of tallgrass prairie, replaced with intensive agriculture. Gone, too, are the scouring flows in the Platte River. The amount of water flowing past Grand Island has been reduced to about one quarter of historic flows. The reduction in mean annual flows is due primarily to diversions for irrigation and hydropower generation. This has transformed the river from an

open, unobstructed, braided riverbed to a floodplain forest
dominated by cottonwood trees with narrow rivulets meandering
through. About 70% of the open river channel is gone. Extensive
forest development has negatively impacted crane roosting
habitat and nesting habitat for Least Terns and Piping Plovers.
Wet meadows, which once bordered the Platte River throughout
its entire length, have been reduced by 75% with the advent of
the plow. Species that evolved in the prairie are challenged by
relatively sudden, dramatic changes in their habitat. On the
other hand, species adapted to woodland areas have benefited
from these changes.

Upland cover types in the Rainwater Basin have changed as well.
Cornfields have replaced the tallgrass prairie. About 90% of the
4,000 original major wetlands have been destroyed through
draining and filling for agricultural purposes and road
construction. Nearly all of the smaller wetlands have been lost
due to land-leveling or drainage. Consequently, our waterfowl
resource is now forced to concentrate in the remaining habitat.
Crowding sets the stage for potentially catastrophic disease
outbreaks and natural disasters. Indeed, avian cholera takes its
toll on ducks and geese each spring, the worst of which occurred
in 1980 when nearly 100,000 waterfowl died as they headed north
to their ancestral nesting grounds. In March 1990, a powerful
low pressure cell spawned tornados and devastating hail storms
during the peak of migration, killing tens of thousands of ducks
and geese. At the turn-of-the-century, there were nearly 100,000
acres of Rainwater Basin wetlands. By 1983, only 21,000 acres
remained, 12,000 of which are now under public ownership.

PLANNING YOUR TRIP

The best time to go birding is "whenever you can." For most
people, Sandhill Cranes are the main attraction, which means
March through early April is the prime time. Weather and water
largely dictate which areas are accessible and are holding birds.
Early in the season it is not unusual for many of the wetlands and
portions of the Platte River to be frozen. Check with the
Rainwater Basin Wetland District (see *Local Contacts*) to find out
what the water conditions are like and which areas are holding
the most waterfowl. Water conditions vary dramatically from
year to year along with drought cycles. If you arrive during wet
weather, the gravel roads can become impassable so use caution.
If you are unsure about a road, don't go down it. Getting stuck
puts a damper on your outing.

FOOD/LODGING- Kearney and Grand Island offer dozens of
fast food stops and restaurants ranging from steak houses to
Mexican and Chinese cuisine. The Coney Island Lunch Room in
Grand Island offers a colorful relief from the monotony of fast food
joints. Both towns also have numerous motels. The Interstate
Holiday Inn in Grand Island and Ramada Inn in Kearney often
give special rates to crane-watchers. These facilities host various
crane-related celebrations each March and are very helpful to
birders. Several campgrounds can be found in the area as well. A
Nebraska Park sticker is required for entry to state wayside and
recreation areas. Primitive camping is allowed on state wildlife
areas without a park sticker. Be sure to obey posted regulations.
The Nebraska Game & Parks Commission will send you a list of
areas (see *Local Contacts*).

PESTS- A birder's guide is not complete without a section on
pests. Ticks, mosquitos, chiggers, deer flies, and biting gnats
round out the list of "insect" pests. Mid-April through June is the

worst time for most of these creatures; however, mosquitos persist until a hard frost in October. Ticks and chiggers taper off in July as the heat of the summer sets in. Wood ticks and Lone Star ticks occur here; the former outnumbering the latter 20 to 1 (this ratio is based on their frequency when I remove them from my dogs). Lyme's disease has been confirmed in Nebraska so use precautions to avoid ticks. Long pants and insect repellent help to discourage ticks, but it is very important that you search your body after walking in brushy areas. Ticks like to burrow in at the back of your neck in particular. Carefully remove ticks by pulling gently on them until they let loose. Chiggers prefer the more open grassy areas. They tend to bite around the socks and waist, where your clothing is more constricted. Itching red welts is a sure sign of chiggers.

Beware of poison ivy and stinging nettles as well. Nettles are found only in wet areas along riparian zones and occur from May until frost. The chances are you will not encounter nettles. On the other hand, poison ivy blankets many riparian areas. Avoid contact with your skin and you should be okay.

Rattlesnakes are extremely rare in this area and it is highly unlikely that you will be fortunate enough to see one. The only species found here is the prairie rattlesnake. I have never seen one here and reports are very infrequent.

BIRDING AREAS BY COUNTY

The seven counties covered in this guide concentrate on the Platte River and Rainwater Basin. Only a few selected areas are identified in each county, leaving the more adventuresome to discover their own "hotspots." Certain areas naturally attract a greater diversity of birds because they offer an oasis in a sea of intensive agriculture. Obviously, the larger wetland areas and the Platte River basin offer the greatest diversity of habitat; however, there are many smaller sites that have potential for producing surprises. Good out-of-the-way places to find birds include shelterbelts, cemeteries, any river or creek drainage, and patches of native prairie.

The following account of counties is by no means a comprehensive treatise on birding spots but it does provide persons unfamiliar with the area some excellent places to begin their exploration of the region.

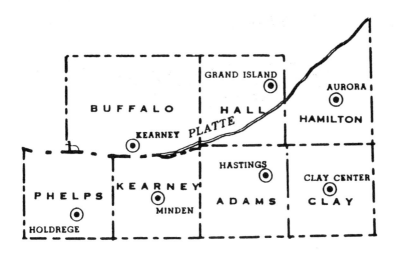

Northern Harrier over Senkiwich's general store. Crane Creek, Hamilton Co. J. W. Wilson '84

ADAMS COUNTY

1) AYR LAKE is a large basin located 3.5 miles south and .5 miles west of the Highway 6 Bypass junction east of Hastings. It is a seasonal wetland which is best noted for shorebirds and wading birds, and, to a lesser extent, waterfowl. April and May are the best times to find American Golden-Plovers, American Avocets, and a host of other species. This is a private basin thus access is restricted.

2) THIRTY-TWO MILE CREEK WATERSHED hosts large numbers of geese and other waterfowl. At times, avian cholera outbreaks affect this basin. March is best for geese. The mudflats attract shorebirds in the spring. The county roads on the west and north side of the impoundment provide good access for viewing.

3) HASTINGS CEMETERY on the east side of Hastings, offers mature cottonwoods and a stream meandering through. Late April and early May can be extremely productive for warblers, vireos, Indigo Buntings, a variety of sparrows, and Rose-breasted Grosbeaks.

4) SUSAN O. HAIL GRAVE STATE HISTORICAL MARKER honors a pioneer woman who died while traveling the Oregon Trail and was buried here in 1852. Wagon ruts are still visible north of the grave. This is a good area to reflect as you look down upon the river valley.

5) LITTLE BLUE RIVER is the dominant drainage feature in the southern portion of the county. In many areas, the riparian zone is lined with cottonwood trees and hackberries with a dense understory. These sites provide attract migrating passerines in the spring and fall. Early May and September are the best times.

6) KENESAW LAGOON is a private basin bordered by tree plantings. Large numbers of waterfowl can be found here in the spring. A small Great Blue Heron colony exists on the east side of the area. Eight Whooping Cranes visited this site for a few days in April 1994. The mudflat area on the southwest side attracts shorebirds, waterfowl, and waders in the spring. Viewing is best from the county roads on the west or south side of the lagoon.

BUFFALO COUNTY

1) LILLIAN ANNETTE ROWE SANCTUARY or "Rowe

Sanctuary" is owned and managed by the National Audubon
Society. It is located along the Platte River south of I-80 between
the Highway 10 Exit #279 and the Gibbon Exit #285. The
headquarters of this 2,200-acre preserve is located 2 miles south
and 2 miles west of the Gibbon Exit. This area is best noted for
its roosting densities of Sandhill Cranes and waterfowl. There
are several observation blinds overlooking the river which are
open to the public on a reservation basis only. March and early
April are best for cranes. Wintering flocks of Mallards and
Canada Geese attract Bald Eagles and occasionally Ferruginous
Hawks from December through March. Bobolink, Dickcissel, and
Upland Sandpiper nest on the meadows from May to August.
Rose-breasted Grosbeak, Willow Flycatcher, and Bell's Vireo nest
along the riparian shrub/woodland community. Least Terns and
Piping Plovers occasionally nest on the sandbars here as well.
You must contact the manager prior to entry.

2) COTTONMILL CITY PARK offers a variety of habitats.

Marsh-like wetland habitat bordered by trees and shrubs attract
several species of songbirds and waterbirds particularly in late
April and May.

3) BASSWAY STRIP STATE WILDLIFE MANAGEMENT

AREA covers 636 acres and is managed by the Nebraska Game
and Parks Commission. It includes 7 miles of river front along
the north channel of the Platte River and is heavily forested.
Access is about 1/2 mile south and east of Minden Exit #279. This
area primarily hosts woodland species and is *not* used by Sandhill
Cranes.

4) BLUE HOLE STATE WILDLIFE MANAGEMENT AREA covers 539 on both sides of the highway south of I-80 Exit #257 (Elm Creek).

The Nebraska Public Power District has created a nesting island for Least Terns and Piping Plovers on the east side of the area. Most of the ground is covered by a mature cottonwood forest. Bald Eagles patrol the river in winter. Look and listen for Bell's Vireo on the willow islands on both sides of the Platte River bridge. The old sandpit lakes attract a variety of diving ducks and an occasional Common Loon has been recorded here. Beaver activity is evident and a large lodge can be seen on the west side of the area.

CLAY COUNTY

CLAY COUNTY lies in the heart of the Rainwater Basin and has numerous wetlands, all of which are good when water conditions are favorable. The hard-surfaced road west of Clay Center offers excellent viewing of field-feeding geese during the spring. Raptors such as Golden Eagles and Prairie Falcons have been seen here. A few black-tailed prairie dog towns exist in the old U.S. Ammunitions Depot and mule deer are occasionally observed also.

1) HARVARD MARSH WATERFOWL PRODUCTION AREA (WPA) encompasses 1,480 acres of federally-owned

marsh. Maximum densities of over 200,000 geese occur here, with numbers peaking in mid-March. Among the hordes of snow geese, the skilled observer will likely find Ross' Geese. About 2-4% of the "white" geese using the basins are Ross'. Late February to early April is the best time to visit. This area consistently produces Cinnamon Teal. Access is difficult during wet weather due to the "gumbo" soils. A small dike offers good viewing during dry weather. Access to the dike is from the west or southwest. If in doubt about driving in, get out and walk! Once you're stuck, getting out is no fun. Short-eared Owls and Northern Harriers can be seen "floating" over the grasslands. This is a good shorebird area from April through August during years of good water conditions. American Avocets have nested here at least once in the past ten years.

2)   MASSIE WPA encompasses about 670 acres. Its

avifauna is similar to Harvard Marsh. Huge numbers of waterfowl are the main attraction. A hiking trail and parking area can be accessed from the south. The brushy areas near the parking area attract a variety of sparrows in the spring including American Tree Sparrows and Harris' Sparrows. Northern

Harriers and Short-eared Owls can be found in the grasslands bordering the marsh. Bald Eagles are attracted to the waterfowl concentrations in the spring as well.

3) SMITH WPA can be an excellent place for waders and waterfowl in some years. This 397-acre basin has a variety habitats and is best covered on foot, although there are no permanent hiking trails.

Horned Lark
Taylor Ranch
© W.S. Whitney

HALL COUNTY

1) MORMON ISLAND CRANE MEADOWS (MICM) is

owned and managed by the Platte River Whooping Crane
Maintenance Trust and covers about 2,500 acres. MICM lies 1
mile south of I-80 Exit #312 near Grand Island. It hosts one of
the densest Sandhill Crane populations on the Platte River. Over
70,000 cranes have been observed foraging on the wet meadows,
and roosting densities number over 80,000 during peak use in late
March and early April. The bird list now stands at 217 species as
of 14 February 1994. Sedge meadows and tallgrass prairie
blankets the area. High densities of Upland Sandpipers,
Dickcissels, Bobolinks, Grasshopper Sparrows, and Sedge Wrens
nest here during May through August. A public observation blind
for viewing cranes and waterfowl is available by reservation from
5 March through 7 April by calling the Crane Meadows Nature
Center (see *Local Contacts*). Access to the property at other times
of the year is by permission only.

2) SHOEMAKER ISLAND ROAD traverses 6 miles across

Shoemaker Island south of I-80 Exits 305 and 300. Large
expanses of sedge meadow and lowland prairie habitat attract
tens of thousands of Sandhill Cranes in March and early April.
American Woodcock perform their courtship rituals along the
wooded river drainage in April and May. The habitat and
avifauna is very similar to MICM. Eastern Wood-Pewee and
Black-headed x Rose-breasted Grosbeak hybrids inhabit the
wooded channel south of the road. A small channel crosses the
road about 1 mile west of the east end. The downstream pool
attracts a variety of songbirds during the summer months where
they bathe and drink. In some years, Greater Prairie-Chickens
occupy a "booming" ground on this island and can be seen
occasionally. Use of this "dancing" ground is irregular. Eastern
Bluebirds nest in boxes erected for them. The south channel is a

major crane roost and Least Terns and Piping Plovers nest on the barren sandbars. Watch for Bald Eagles perched in cottonwoods from late November through March. All of this area is private land and permission must be obtained to enter, although much can be seen along the road. Brushy areas attract wintering Harris' Sparrows and American Tree Sparrows while the meadows harbor Rough-legged Hawks, Northern Harriers, Northern Shrikes, and Short-eared Owls. There is a pull-off overlooking the south channel less than a few hundred yards south of the intersection of Shoemaker Island Road and Alda Road. This is a good area to watch roosting cranes from a distance.

3) NINE-MILE BRIDGE is a great place to view roosting Sandhill Cranes at dusk or dawn. Parking is a problem here so use caution.

4) CORNHUSKER STATE WILDLIFE AREA totals 814 acres in 3 separate parcels. The brushy shelterbelts adjacent to weedy fields are good places to find Harris' Sparrows and other passerines. It probably isn't worth spending much time here unless you really need a Harris' or American Tree Sparrow on your list.

5) CRANE MEADOWS NATURE CENTER is located .5 miles south of I-80 Exit #305 (Alda). The 240-acre area features nearly five miles of hiking trails and is open year-around. A bluebird box trail is just one of many activities available to the public. This island area features a variety of grassland nesting species such as Bobolink and Upland Sandpiper, and it has a thriving population of Wild Turkeys. Field Sparrows and Black-billed Magpies nest on the property. A bird-feeding station located near the building, attracts a wide variety of species including Harris' Sparrow, Rufous-sided Towhee, American

Goldfinches, American Tree Sparrows, Chipping Sparrows, Clay-colored Sparrows, and even a Northern Mockingbird on occasion. Willow Flycatcher and Bell's Vireo nest along the north channel. River otters have been reintroduced along the Platte and this site hosts a viable population. The native prairie features an astounding array of wildflowers as well.

6) HALL COUNTY PARK abuts the south side of the Stuhr Museum. Its entrance is .5 miles east of Hwy 281 on Schimmer Road. Late April through May is a good time to stroll through this 59-acre wooded area. Warblers, thrushes, and Rose-breasted Grosbeaks are found here at that time and offer a nice addition to the prairie species. Long-eared Owls have infrequently wintered in the past as well. Entrance is free and there is a marked hiking trail. Telephone (308) 381-5087.

7) TAYLOR RANCH is a privately owned 7,000-acre ranch and is not open to the public. The area is a remnant Sandhills prairie with scattered wetlands and is largely unplowed. It hosts a resident flock of Greater Prairie-Chickens with a few Sharp-tailed Grouse mixed in. Eighty species have been observed here. Ross' Geese, Cinnamon Teal, and Pied-billed Grebes are among the spring visitors. These species can be viewed from the county roads. The county line trail (Loup River Road) on the north side of the property is a great trail to explore but it is not recommended for passenger cars. Several booming grounds can be located by the alert observer by stopping at 1/4 mile intervals and listening. The best time is April and May. Blue Grosbeaks apparently nest near the plum thickets. A shooting preserve adjoins this ranch and Chukars are released on that preserve so don't be surprised to see one. However, they don't count on your list!

HAMILTON COUNTY

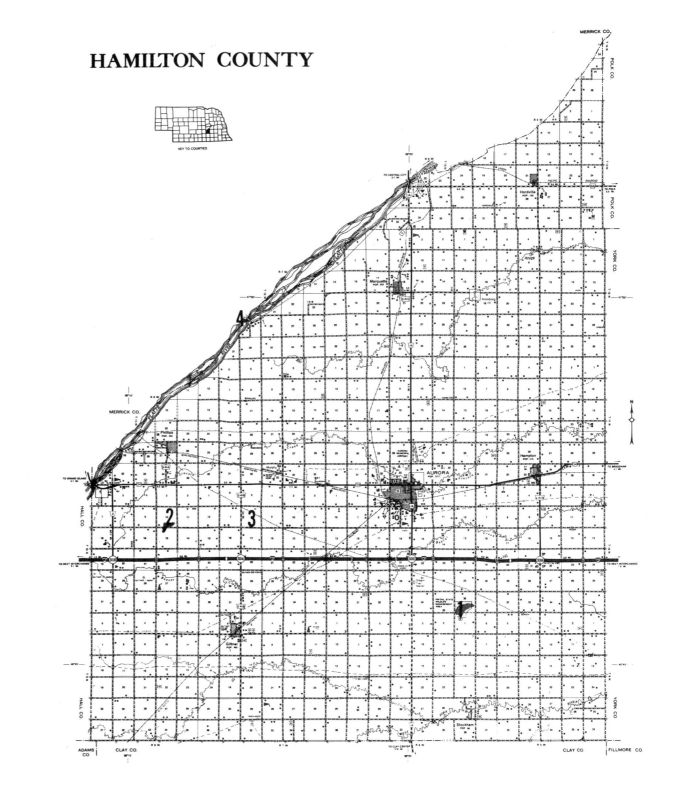

HAMILTON COUNTY

1) PINTAIL STATE WILDLIFE AREA covers 283 acres and is located 2.5 miles south and 2 miles east of I-80 Exit #332 (Aurora). Over 100,000 geese, primarily Greater Snow Geese, occur here during peak use in mid-March. Shorebirds, waders, American White Pelicans, Black Terns, and other waterfowl species rest here during spring migration.

2) DEEP WELL STATE WILDLIFE AREA lies 1.5 miles north and 2.5 miles east of I-80 Exit #318. It is known locally as the Phillips Basin. Mudflats and emergent vegetation harbor Semipalmated Plover, Marbled Godwit, Willet, Black Tern, and a host of other waterbirds during May. Waterfowl concentrations peak in mid-March. Yellow-headed Blackbirds occasionally nest in the emergent vegetation as do Pied-billed Grebes. A King Rail was seen here in 1992. The best viewing is from the road on the south side of the wetland. Common Yellowthroats, Yellow Warblers, and Yellow-rumped Warblers can be seen as well.

3) SPRINGER WPA was purchased in 1991 as a joint venture between the U.S. Fish & Wildlife Service and Ducks Unlimited. It represents the first major restoration project in the Rainwater Basin and contains 480 acres.

4) BADER MEMORIAL PARK lies within Merrick County on the border of Hamilton County. This park is a county-operated area comprising some 200 acres of Platte River woodlands, shrublands, and prairie grasslands. An 80-acre portion of this property is set aside as a natural area. Hiking trails meander through a variety of habitats and an interpretive guide to the flora and fauna of the site is available from Prairie Plains Resource Institute (see *Local Contacts*). This area is near the western limit of nesting American Woodcock. Over 130 species of birds have been recorded here. Bell's Vireo, Warbling Vireo, and Cedar Waxing are a few of the nesting species. In early summer, Regal Fritillaries and other butterflies "dance" among the wild prairie flowers. There is also a healthy population of beaver and white-tailed deer.

KEARNEY COUNTY

KEY TO COUNTIES

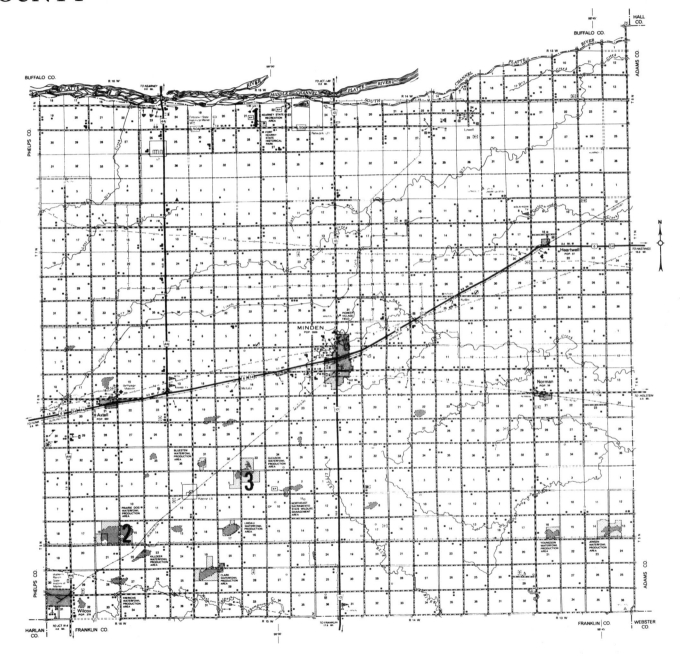

KEARNEY COUNTY

1) FORT KEARNY STATE HISTORICAL PARK AND RECREATION AREA located 3 miles south and 4 miles west of

I-80 Exit #272 (Kearney), offers a public Hike Bike Trail which crosses the Platte River and is good viewing for cranes in the spring and other birds throughout the year. The fort has an interpretive center and concession area. Photography blinds for cranes can be reserved. A state park sticker is required for entry. Woody undergrowth attracts a variety of riparian woodland species including Bell's Vireo and Indigo Bunting. The drive to the area in March will take you through field after field of feeding cranes and geese.

2) PRAIRIE DOG WPA is 5.5 miles south of Axtell. Spring

waterfowl concentrations are the drawing card for this 811-acre area. A small black-tailed prairie dog town is located on the higher ground east of the road near the small red cedars. This and the surrounding basins attract large numbers of Greater White-fronted Geese and several subspecies of Canada Geese. Whooping Cranes have been observed here in April and it is a great place for waders and shorebirds in late spring and late summer.

3) GLEASON WPA is slightly smaller than Prairie Dog WPA,

covering 569 acres. It offers a good variety of waterfowl, waders, and shorebirds. The best viewing is south of the east-west county road which bisects the area. White-faced Ibis, Pectoral Sandpipers, Black-crowned Night-Herons, and Whooping Cranes have been reported here in past years.

PHELPS COUNTY

KEY TO COUNTIES

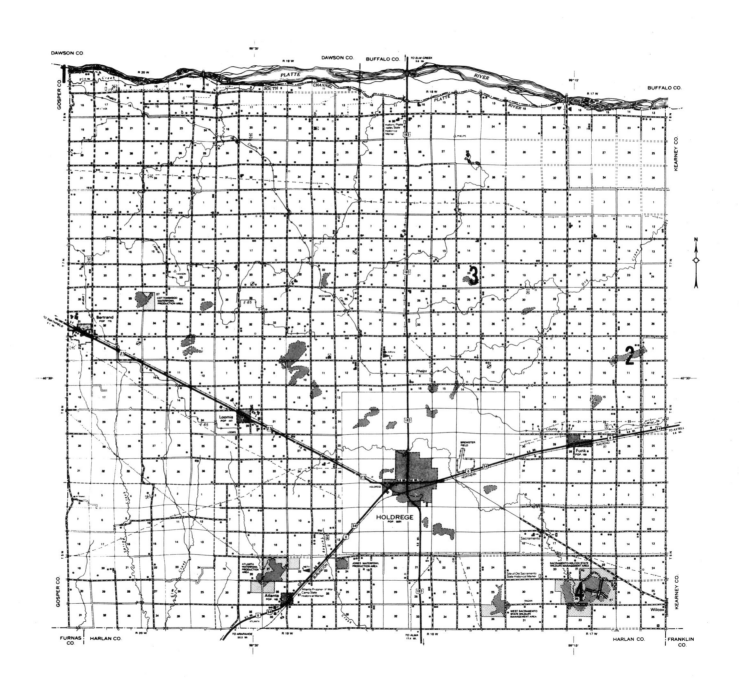

PHELPS COUNTY

1) PLATTE RIVER ROAD near Jeffrey's Island

is found by taking I-80 Exit #248 (Overton) south to the "T"
(there's a stop sign there) then head west 4.5 miles on the
blacktop, then north 1 mile on the gravel road which turns west
next to the Platte River. The next 2 miles (1 mile of which is in
Gosper County) runs right along the river and offers excellent
birding throughout the year. The north side of the river is
Jeffrey's Island which is in Dawson County. A large Great Blue
Heron colony exists in the trees on the north channel. This reach
hosts over 100 Bald Eagles during the winter months and affords
an excellent view of our national symbol. Least Terns and Piping
Plovers nest within this 2-mile reach and a large variety of
shorebirds pass through, including Stilt Sandpipers and Western
Sandpipers. Eastern Bluebirds and Blue Grosbeaks inhabit the
open scrub just east of the canal overpass. Forster's Terns feed in
this reach during migration.

2) FUNK LAGOON WPA is a 1,977-acre federally-owned

marsh found 1 mile east and 3 miles north of Funk. It is one of
the few basins with permanent water and has some of the best
marsh vegetation. Yellow-headed Blackbirds and Great-tailed
Grackles nest in the cattails. Those of you with tapes should be
able to get responses from Sora and Virginia Rail. This is a good
area for a variety of waders including Black-crowned
Night-Heron. Cinnamon Teal regularly occur in the spring in
addition to tens of thousands of geese and ducks. American White
Pelicans, Double-crested Cormorants, and Eared Grebes can be
seen in the deep water areas and Whooping Cranes have roosted
here during April and October.

3) JOHNSON WPA is another federally-owned area of

nearly 500 acres, 9 miles south and 2.5 miles east of I-80 Exit

#257 (Elm Creek). The mudflats on the west side are excellent for shorebirds. Whooping Cranes and Peregrine Falcons have been seen here during migration. Waterfowl and waterbirds are abundant.

4) SACRAMENTO STATE WILDLIFE MANAGEMENT AREA has several controlled water impoundments and numerous tree and shrub plantings extending over 3,000 acres. The headquarters is located on the east side of the area about 2 miles west and 1/2 mile north of Wilcox. A wide variety of bird life can be found. Winter roosts of Long-eared Owls have been reported in the past.

SPECIALTIES OF THE REGION

THE MAIN ATTRACTIONS

SANDHILL CRANE- Based on fossil records, cranes have been part of the Nebraska landscape for ten million years, long before there was a Platte River. Sandhill Cranes attract birders to this area from all over the world, and crane-watching has become a major tourist industry. Huge flocks can be seen within the

Sandhill Cranes
©'94 Wm.S.Whitney

45-mile reach between Kearney and Grand Island, and the air resonates with their calls. A few begin to arrive around Valentine's Day and the first mass exodus occurs around April 10. In past years, a few have wintered in the area. The peak of migration occurs from March 20 through April 5 when over 250,000 cranes may be seen. At night the cranes roost in the security of the Platte's shallow waters, numbering over 15,000 cranes per 1/2 mile of river. Near dusk the flocks descend upon the river offering a sight that is sure to send shivers down your spine. At dawn the cranes leave the roost and head to nearby fields where they spend the day feeding, preening, and dancing. One 1,000-acre wet meadow held 70,000 cranes during peak use. Great kettles of soaring cranes appear as wisps of smoke during the middle of sunny days. They are apparently testing the air currents and keeping their flight muscles tuned as they prepare for their northward departure. They generally remain within 5 miles of the river and can be easily observed along any of the county roads that parallel the river.

CRANE-WATCHING ETIQUETTE

1. Cranes need to be allowed to feed and roost undisturbed for their safety and well-being.

2. Your car is an effective blind for viewing cranes. Remain in or near your car for best viewing. Drive carefully.

3. Cranes are extremely wary of persons afoot and should not be approached. Leave them undisturbed.

4. Nearly all area land is Private Property. Remember that trespassing is inconsiderate and illegal.

5. Observe posted regulations and do not stop on bridges or interstate

If you look closely, you will notice that family groups make up the larger flocks. Families consist of both adults, which pair for life, and last year's colt or chick. The youngsters have a unique "peep" call which can be heard especially during flight. There are 3 subspecies of cranes which occur here; the Greater, the Canadian or Intermediate, and the Lesser Sandhill Crane. As their names suggest, they can be distinguished by size, height, and bill length. The Arctic-nesting Lessers are the smallest, followed by the intermediate-sized Canadians, and the four-foot tall Greaters. In terms of abundance, the Lesser makes up at least 80% of the population while the Greater makes up only about 5%. An

individual crane will spend about 28 days on the Platte and will
gain over 1/2 pound of fat. Corn makes up 90% of their diet.
They glean the fields for waste corn left from fall's harvest. About
1,600 tons of corn are consumed by the cranes. The remaining
10% of their diet is animal matter including insect larvae,
earthworms, and snails. This vital dietary component can only be
found in the wet meadows and native grasslands bordering the
Platte. In some areas they ingest stone-like nodules composed of
calcium carbonate which provides the cranes with important
minerals. On a typical day, a crane will travel 6 miles, returning
to the same roost site at night. When the Platte is frozen, cranes
will roost on wet meadows or on the ice but they prefer the
shallow waters of the Platte. Every year there are one or two
partial albino Sandhill Cranes sighted, so make sure you rule out
this possibility before you add Whooping Crane to your list.
A number of organizations sponsor tours and have blinds
available on a reservation basis (see *Local Contacts*). Guided
tours generally run from 5 March through 7 April. If you decide
to witness the roosting flights on your own, you should plan to
arrive at your destination at least 45 minutes *before* sunrise or
sunset. A sunrise/sunset schedule is included for your
convenience. Due to the traffic hazards and concern for safety at
some of the bridge crossings, it is not advisable to park along the
road right-of-way or walk onto any of the highway bridges.
Please read and observe the crane-watching etiquette section for
your own personal safety and enjoyment. During adverse
weather, it is advisable to remain on hard-surfaced roads such as
the Platte River Road west of Doniphan in Hall County or the
road past Ft. Kearny State Historical Park in Kearney County. A
major crane staging area that has not received the publicity given
the Big Bend reach of the Platte is a site east of Hershey along
the North Platte River in Lincoln County. Peak numbers of
100,000 cranes have been recorded here. Contact the North
Platte Field Office of the Nebraska Game & Parks Commission for

more information. Fall migration is more prolonged in time and space as the cranes trickle through Nebraska accompanied by colts less than 6 months old. Peak numbers are less than 10,000 cranes in the fall. The last half of October is the best time to find cranes in the region during fall, although it is no comparison to the spring.

Sunrise/Sunset Table

Date	March Rise	March Set	April* Rise	April* Set
1	7:08	6:24	6:17	6:58
5	7:02	6:29	6:11	7:02
10	6:54	6:34	6:03	7:07
15	6:46	6:40	5:55	7:13
20	6:37	6:45	5:47	7:18
25	6:29	6:50	5:40	7:23
30	6:21	6:56	5:33	7:28

* Time is in Central Standard Time (CST). Note: time changes to Central Daylight Time (CDT) the first Sunday in April.

WATERFOWL- The Platte River valley and Rainwater Basin host nearly ten million ducks and geese each year. Greater White-fronted Geese, Snow Geese, Canada Geese, Mallard, Northern Pintail, American Wigeon, Northern Shoveler, Blue-winged Teal, and Green-winged Teal are the predominant species. Others include Ross' Goose, Gadwall, Cinnamon Teal, Ring-necked Duck, Lesser Scaup, Redhead, Canvasback, Common Merganser, and Ruddy Duck. Ninety percent (over a quarter million) of the mid-continent flock of Greater White-fronted Geese stage in the area each spring. The largest concentrations occur from mid-February to early April. When the basins are frozen they will congregate along the Platte in the same general area as Sandhill Cranes. When the ice melts and open-water areas

become available, the birds return to the Rainwater Basin
wetlands. Some of the basins support huge numbers of migrating
waterfowl. At Harvard Marsh, a 760-acre wetland in Clay
County, peak use has approached 500,000 geese and ducks. Prior
to 1981, Snow Geese were rare in the area. Today they are the
most numerous species of goose and may exceed one million
individuals at peak. Both white and blue phases are present.
Look over the vast flocks carefully and you may be rewarded by
finding the smaller Ross' Goose. About 2-4% of the "white" geese
out there are Ross' Geese. An exciting discovery would be to find
a "blue" phase Ross' Goose. Avid waterfowlers will marvel at the
size variation of the several races of Canada Geese that may be
observed in common flocks. The small Cackling race is slightly

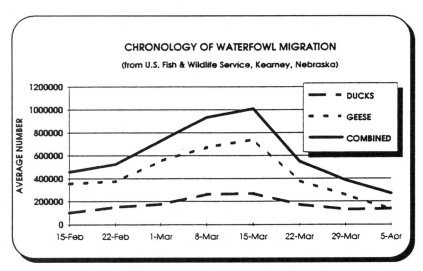

larger than a Mallard while the Giant race reaches 14 pounds.
Ducks can be seen in full nuptial plumage in the scattered
wetlands. Courtship flights of Northern Pintails offer a study in
aerial acrobatics as several drakes chase a hen. Some of the best
wetlands for viewing waterfowl are Harvard Marsh, Massie
Waterfowl Production Area (WPA), Pintail State Wildlife Area,
Funk WPA, and Gleason WPA. Mallard, Wood Duck, and

Blue-winged Teal are the most common nesting species in the area. The fall migration can produce large numbers of waterfowl (although nothing like the spring) but the hunting season makes viewing undisturbed birds more difficult. Several thousand Canada Geese and Mallards winter along portions of the Platte River. An excellent area to view geese during the winter is at the sandpit near Grandpa's Steak House south of I-80 in Kearney. During the winter watch for Bald Eagles perched in cottonwoods overlooking waterfowl concentrations.

THREATENED AND ENDANGERED SPECIES

BALD EAGLE- Winter is when to see Bald Eagles in Nebraska. Although the Occurrence Table shows them year-around, the best time to find them is from late October through the third week of

Bald Eagle raids Borgeson Basin   Schauer · 94

March. Peak numbers occur from late February through mid-March as migrants join winter residents along open stretches of river. Central Nebraska Public Power and Irrigation District offers guided eagle viewing southeast of Lexington and at Lake McConaughy. In late February 1994, over 350 Bald Eagles congregated below the Kingsley Dam at Lake McConaughy where they gorged on alewifes, a species of fish. Typically about 200 eagles winter along the Big Bend reach of the Platte. Bald Eagles have been observed building nests at several locations within the state but it wasn't until 1991 that eggs were laid. There are about 21 known nest sites within the state as of 1994. Eagles can be observed rather easily along the Platte River especially southwest of the Overton Exit #248. Look for them in early March patrolling large flocks of waterfowl at any of the Rainwater Basin wetlands. A good indication of the presence of an eagle is a

sudden up-flight of resting geese. As the mass takes flight, you will likely find the telltale silhouette of an eagle looking for food. They readily feed on waterfowl which have died due to avian

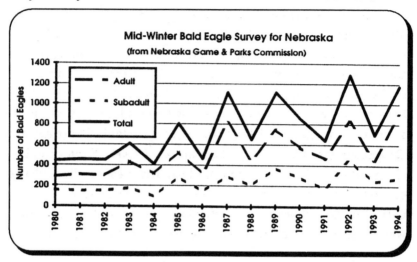

cholera. Their digestive physiology is such that they are immune to the *Pasturella multicida* bacteria which kills the ducks and geese.

PEREGRINE FALCON- Your best chances to see a rare Peregrine Falcon is in the spring. Recent reintroduction efforts in Omaha have met with some success so the prospect for finding one in the future is improving. All of the Peregrines I have seen were associated with wetlands, whether in the Rainwater Basin or the Platte River. Their size and stature make them a formidable predator of waterfowl and shorebirds in particular. Any sighting of this falcon is a noteworthy event so consider yourself lucky if you happen upon one.

WHOOPING CRANE- If you long to see Whooping Cranes in the wild, go to Aransas National Refuge in Texas where they winter. The chances of seeing this species in Nebraska is very slim yet they occur here twice a year during migration. Dates of occurrence are 17 March to 15 May and 22 September to 3 December. Peak migration occurs 1-20 April and 20-31 October. Critical habitat for this endangered species has been designated along a 53-mile reach of the Platte River from the Shelton Bridge to the Lexington Bridge. The reach between Wood River and Hwy 10 has the most consistent use. Several of the Rainwater Basin wetlands in Kearney and Phelps counties have consistent use as well, such as Funk, Johnson's, Prairie Dog, and Gleason. Most occurrences are one-night stays thus whoopers are difficult to "stake-out". However, it is not unusual for family groups to spend several days in the area during the fall migration. The length of stay record during migration occurred along the Platte in spring 1987 when an individual stayed 34 days. Thousands of

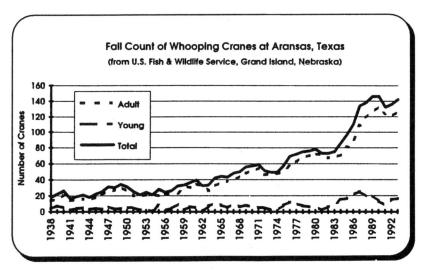

people were able to view this bird and it was not uncommon to see school buses pulled over for a short pause to watch this crane. This area's historic importance to Whooping Cranes is evident since Nebraska has the dubious distinction of having more "kill" records than any other place on the North American continent. Although their numbers have increased since the 1940's, they are still critically endangered.

PIPING PLOVER AND LEAST TERN- Both of these federally listed species nest on the barren sandbars of the Platte River and on several adjacent sandpits. Arrival dates range from 13-20 April for plovers and 27 April to 10 May for terns. Nest initiation dates are from 3 May to 28 June and from 22 May to 24 July for plovers and terns respectively. The peak of nesting is the first half of June for both species. Piping Plovers depart by 15 August while Least Terns depart by 4 September. Terns congregate at post-nesting dispersal areas for 2 to 4 weeks beginning in mid-July. As many as 25 terns have been observed at these sites. One such area is at the Highway 34 bridge southeast of Grand

Piping Plover Nest
© '94 Wm.S.Whitney

Island. Both species may occasionally be seen foraging near the
Alda bridge pull-off 2 miles south of I-80 Exit #305. Another
foraging area is located downstream from the Highway 44 bridge
south of Kearney (I-80 Exit #272). These sites may or may not be
used in any given year. It is unlawful to disturb these birds while
they are nesting, so avoid posted areas. The Platte River
Whooping Crane Trust and the Nebraska Public Power District
(NPPD) manage sites specifically for these species. Contact the
Platte River Whooping Trust or NPPD (see *Local Contacts*) about
the possibility of seeing these birds in June or early July.

ESKIMO CURLEW- In the latter part of the 19th Century, the
Eskimo Curlew was present in tremendous numbers as a spring
migrant through the Great Plains enroute to their Arctic nesting
grounds in northwest Canada. Adams, Buffalo, Hall, Hamilton,
York, and Fillmore counties apparently served as a major
migration stop-over area for this species from early April to late
May. Fred Stolley, a farmer near Grand Island, recalled flocks of
500 to 1000 curlews gathering at newly-plowed fields in the
1860s. In mid-afternoon, great flocks would spiral into the sky,
nearly out of sight, circling and calling. The curlews were
relatively tame and were extremely vulnerable to hunters who
shot them by the wagonload to sell to eastern markets. Many
loads spoiled enroute to the market and piles of rotting birds were
dumped on the prairie so that hunters could refill the wagons. By
1890, such slaughters had significantly reduced their populations.
The last known specimen taken in Nebraska was near Hastings
in April 1926. Today, they may be extinct although isolated
sightings of these rare shorebirds are reported each decade. The
most recent report was 16 April 1987, when one bird was reported
on Mormon Island Crane Meadows 10 miles south of Grand
Island. Unfortunately, no photograph was taken. Specimens are
currently housed at the University of Nebraska State Museum in
Lincoln and at the Hastings Museum.

OTHER SPECIES OF HIGH INTEREST

WADERS- The most abundant wader is the Great Blue Heron. Several large colonies exist along the Platte River and this species is increasing as a nesting bird. Their large stick nests at the tops of cottonwoods are conspicuous during the winter months. They return to their colonies the last half of April to begin the nesting season. About 12 nest platforms were visible on the south side of I-80 about 3/8 mile east of mile-marker (mm) #310 for the past five years. Green Herons nest along the younger riparian woodlands as well, although their nests are far more difficult to locate. There has been an increasing number of Cattle Egrets in the spring and a few Great Egrets which summer here. It is possible that both of these species will establish themselves as nesters in the future. Late July through August is the best time to view waders. Post-nesting dispersal sends several species to this region which typically nest at Cheyenne Bottoms, Kansas and points southward or in surrounding areas. They include Little Blue Heron (9 of 10 will be the white immature plumaged individuals so don't shoot from your hip when you identify a white wader), Snowy Egret, Cattle Egret, White-faced Ibis, and Black-crowned Night-Heron. As with shorebirds, the riverine sandbars and shallow Rainwater Basin wetlands attract multitudes of waders in some years.

RAPTORS- No matter what time of the year you visit, you can't help noticing the abundant birds of prey which occur here. The various color-morphs of Red-tailed Hawks in particular and also of Rough-legged, Swainson's, and Ferruginous hawks will challenge even the most experienced birder. In winter, American Kestrels are most frequently observed, followed closely by Red-tailed Hawks and Bald Eagles. Northern Harriers, Rough-legged and Ferruginous hawks, and Prairie Falcons comprise the bulk of remaining sightings. Look for redtails and

Bald Eagles soaring above or perched along riparian woodlands. Roughlegs and harriers prefer more open country where they search for meadow voles (a small rodent), their primary prey. When snow cover is heavy, Ferruginous Hawks may be seen perched on the edges of cornfields awaiting the evening feeding flights of Mallards. They are powerful hunters and regularly take Mallards only to have their hard-won prey stolen by pirating Bald Eagles. This drama repeats itself night after night during some winters. Harriers float above the prairie meadows by day and Short-eared Owls come out at dusk, coursing the meadows like giant butterflies as they stalk their prey. One evening in early November I observed 15 harriers and 4 Short-eared Owls cart-wheeling and careening against a blazing red sunset above Mormon Island Crane Meadows. These two species roost, and occasionally nest, in the tall grassy areas of the Rainwater Basin or wet meadows along the Platte. Golden Eagles and Prairie Falcons inhabit the more open country as well and are often seen in the Rainwater Basin. Both of these latter species, as well as Ferruginous Hawks, nest in the western part of the state. Subadult goldens outnumber adults five to one here. Winter is when Northern Goshawks may be present. This species is irruptive in their occurrence, moving here when snowshoe hare populations crash. These rather shy birds prefer wooded areas and are difficult to find. From April through September, Swainson's Hawks take over as the most commonly observed raptor outside of the river valley. They nest in shelterbelts and isolated woodlots. This species is a bird of fire, apparently attracted to prescribed burns by the smoke. While conducting prescribed burns in April, I've seen groups of up to ten individuals soaring above the fire, ready to pounce on small mammals fleeing the flames or waiting for the flames to subside to scavenge hapless victims. An often overlooked but ubiquitous denizen of wooded edges is the Great Horned Owl. Courtship begins in early December as pairs hoot to one another, staking out territorial

Swainson's Hawks Over Ratcliff Prairie, Spring "Burn" - E.V.Wilson -94

claims. By late February the pair is incubating in nests often stolen from Red-tailed Hawks. The eggs hatch in late March or early April and the owlets eventually fledge in June. An astute observer will take the time to "glass" all stick nests in the spring. Ear tufts protruding from a rounded head is a telltale sign of an owl on a nest. Eastern Screech-Owls are also very common; however, they are seldom seen. They can easily be found by playing a tape-recording before dawn near a wooded area in either rural or urban settings. Cemeteries, parks, and riparian woodlands are preferred haunts. You will hear the whinnying cry of this small owl answering the tape and if you are lucky they will fly in next to you. Mississippi Kites are irregular summer visitors. Central Kansas is the nearest regular nesting area for this species. Post-nesting dispersal of kites is northward some years so it is not unusual to find kites here in late July through early September. They have been observed on golf courses or along riparian woodlands bordering open grasslands.

SHOREBIRDS- Mid-April through May and again in mid-July through mid-August is the best time to see shorebirds. Killdeer are the first to arrive in March, followed by Greater Yellowlegs and Baird's Sandpipers. In early April, flocks of Semipalmated and Pectoral sandpipers arrive. Least Sandpipers and Lesser Yellowlegs appear in mid-April. In some years, Buff-breasted Sandpipers arrive in fair numbers and are often seen in newly planted cornfields where they seek grubs. By May, the Baird's have left. The last wave of shorebirds are White-rumped Sandpipers, some of which linger until early June. In June, Greater Yellowlegs appear once again on their southward trek. In early July, other species of sandpipers arrive on the scene after their nesting season in the Arctic. Sanderlings, Semipalmated Plovers, and Least Sandpipers are more plentiful during the "fall" migration. In early August, the barren sandbars of the Platte are alive with small groups of shorebirds. By September, most have passed as the cycle prepares to repeat itself next spring. The key to shorebird presence is water conditions, not only locally, but at Cheyenne Bottoms, a spring shorebird staging area of critical importance located 200 miles south in Kansas. During drought years or years of extremely high water, shorebirds will fly over Cheyenne Bottoms and arrive at the Rainwater Basin or Platte River habitats in great numbers. Likewise, if drought conditions persist locally, the basins will be devoid of shorebirds and the sandbars of the Platte become extremely important. Check with the Kearney Wetlands Office regarding water conditions in the basins. Some of the basins have groundwater irrigation pumps and can be flooded if necessary. Gleason WPA can be very productive some years. Other basins are more or less productive, depending on the amount of mudflats.

GREATER PRAIRIE-CHICKEN & SHARP-TAILED GROUSE-

Because of the popularity of these two species, I have included special information in the *Local Contacts* section so that you can make arrangements to view these birds from blinds as they perform their courtship dances during March through May. The heart of the range for both species of "prairie grouse" is the Sandhills, a large grassland region in the northcentral part of Nebraska. However, both species occur within this area. Large expanses of native prairie are necessary for "grouse" to survive. The hilly areas south of the Platte River between Wood River and Kearney offer some habitat. The best place to view these birds in this area is at the Taylor Ranch in northern Hall County. One accessible Greater Prairie-Chicken lek that can be viewed from a county road is located there (see Hall County map). From I-80, head north at Exit #312 (Grand Island) on Highway 281 to Highway 2, turn west on Highway 2 about 4 miles, turn north on 60th Road until you reach a stop sign (about 2.5 miles), then turn west (left) on One R Road and travel exactly 1 mile. Turn your vehicle around so it is facing east and look about 200 yards to the northeast and watch the drama unfold. You will want to arrive there 40 minutes before sunrise and **STAY IN YOUR VEHICLE** so you do not disturb the prairie chickens. The low booming and clucking of these birds can be easily heard if the wind is not too strong. Up to a dozen males have been using this lek at least since 1981. If you are extremely lucky, you may also see some Sharp-tailed Grouse from the same location. Simply look the hills over about 1/2 mile to the south. If they are there, their white tail feathers will flash against the bluestem while they dance. Only about 4 male sharptails have been seen there in the past and they are not always cooperative so do not be disappointed if you miss them. The best time to go is April through early May when the hens arrive on the leks; however, good booming activity begins in March provided there is little or no snow cover. A perfect way to top off a morning of "chicken" viewing is to head north to Dannebrog (10 miles northeast of Cairo) for breakfast or Sunday buffet at Harriet's Danish Restaurant. Their hours are usually from 7 AM until 2 PM. Don't bother calling; they don't have a phone. The home-cooked food is excellent and the atmosphere is uniquely small-town Nebraska. Roger Welsch (*Postcard from Nebraska*) has popularized this quaint community on CBS's *Sunday Morning* with Charles Kuralt. This stop is worthwhile even if you are not chicken-viewing.

UPLAND SANDPIPER- On or about the 20th of April, Upland Sandpipers arrive, fresh from their wintering grounds on the South American pampas. Equally abrupt is their departure in late August. They waste little time initiating their nests; egg dates range from 10 May to 27 June. The male's wolf-whistle call is given in flight. These birds are obligate grassland nesters and are common on the lowland meadows bordering the Platte and in native prairie tracts throughout the region. The maximum count on Mormon Island Crane Meadows was 114 individuals on 5 May 1988. They are attracted to burned areas where they pick and glean for insects and even prairie skinks (a small lizard) which succumb to the fire. Bader Park, the Taylor Ranch, Audubon's Rowe Sanctuary, and Crane Meadows Nature Center are but a few areas where you can find them.

Upland Sandpiper
Mormon Island

©'94   Wm. S. Whitney

AMERICAN WOODCOCK-- Far from its classic northwoods haunts, this diminutive recluse has found a new home along the forested rivers of Nebraska where the male performs his "twitter flight" so eloquently described in Aldo Leopold's *Sand County Almanac*. Generations later, this same courtship ritual is performed along the wooded banks of the Platte River beginning

as early as mid-March and continuing through early May. This
dusk performance goes largely unnoticed to the human eye, but
draws quite an audience among conspecifics. The action begins
from five to twenty minutes after sunset, depending on cloud
conditions (earlier on overcast evenings and later on clear
evenings). For the next 30 minutes or so, the male performs his
display. I have encountered newly hatched chicks in late April
while searching the forest floor for morel mushrooms. Egg-laying
begins in late March. I have observed "peenting" males on the
edge of young forested areas from Bader Park in Merrick County
west to Kearney. Shoemaker Island is a good place as is the
vicinity of the Grand Island skeet range on South Locust Street
3.5 miles south of Grand Island. I have watched courtship flights
in late March among the din of roosting Sandhill Cranes, the
shrill calls of Bald Eagles entering their roost, and the squeals of
hen Wood Ducks. Add to that a chorus of coyotes howling in the
distance for a truly memorable encounter with the "timberdoodle."

MID DAY MEAL - FRANKLIN'S GULLS, PLATTE BLUFFS

FRANKLIN'S GULL- According to Breeding Bird Surveys, this
species has declined by 90% in the last 30 years for reasons not
entirely known. They pass through here in migration and large
flocks can be seen following the corn-planters in late April. In
Utah, this gull is credited with saving the Mormons when
tremendous flocks descended upon their wheatfields, consuming
the locusts which would have surely destroyed their crops. Next
to the Ring-billed Gull, this is the most common species of gull.
They can be found anywhere in the spring but are more closely
associated with wetlands and the Platte during their fall
migration. The only other "black-headed" gull in our area is the
Bonaparte's Gull which is uncommon to rare and never seems to
number more than 7 or 8 individuals in a group.

EV Uhaner-94

BURROWING OWL- Gracing the logo of the Nebraska
Ornithologists' Union, this intriguing owl is uncommon and local
in this area. They are most easily observed in early May when
they are courting and again in July when they are tending young.
The plow and the wholesale slaughter of prairie dogs have done
much to reduce the habitat of Burrowing Owls. Even today, as
archaic as it is, Nebraska law *requires* landowners to "control" (in
other words, kill) prairie dogs so that they do not spread on to the
neighbors land. Be that as it may, some "dog" towns still survive
and some host Burrowing Owls. From Hastings in Adams
County, head east on Highway 6 to Central Community College.
Turn south for 1 mile then head east 1.5 miles. Just before you
reach the stop sign, look to the south and you will see dozens of
black-tailed prairie dog mounds. I don't know if this town has
owls but it is a good place for other raptors. In Phelps County,
head south at I-80 Exit #257 (Elm Creek) 2 miles then turn west
for 4.5 miles and on the south side of the road you will find a large
prairie dog town. This site has had nesting Burrowing Owls in
recent years. Continue west another 2 1/4 miles and look north
just before the intersection at a smaller dog town. Owls have
nested here as well. In Hall County, head 8 miles north on
Highway 281 from I-80 (Exit #312) to 13th Street, turn west for 3
miles then head 1/2 mile north on Monitor Road. The antenna
fields on either side of Monitor has had nesting Burrowing Owls
in past years even though there are no prairie dogs in the area.
Pay particular attention to the east side and carefully look for
owls which may be barely visible in the taller grass. Owls have
also nested at the Central Nebraska Regional Airport northeast of
Grand Island. The Municipal Golf Course on the east side of the
airport property has had owls perched on the fenceposts in some
years. If you are just interested in viewing black-tailed prairie
dogs, you need not look any further than the parking lot of the
I-80 Holiday Inn at Exit #312. Go behind the NTV building and

look west. You will see a couple of large cottonwood trees on a raised area about 200 yards out in the meadow. That raised area supports a small dog town. In Buffalo County, a large prairie dog colony exists just north of Kearney on the west side of Highway 10; however, I do not know if owls occur there.

RED-HEADED WOODPECKER- This striking woodpecker is common in the mature open cottonwood forests of riparian zones, being most abundant from May through early September. This population seems to be thriving, a stark contrast from the population crashes occurring throughout much of the East. I thoroughly enjoy having Red-headed Woodpeckers around and I never tire of playing hide-and-seek with them as they cling to the opposite side of a fencepost or utility pole as you drive slowly by. Aside from competition for nest cavities from European Starlings, the biggest threat to this species is vehicular collisions. Redheads like to "fly-catch" and unfortunately they are oblivious to danger when in pursuit of prey, all too often with fatal results for the bird. During the summer, they are the most common "road-kill" encountered near the Platte River.

NORTHERN FLICKER- When "Yellow-shafted" and "Red-shafted" flickers were lumped to one species in 1983, we lost something. Although it is customary for Christmas Counts to differentiate between the two, all too often they do not. During the summer, it is rare to find a "Red-shafted Flicker." They tend to migrate out of the area leaving only the "Yellow-shafted Flickers" to nest. However, "Red-shafted Flickers" occur here in almost equal numbers during the winter as birds from western populations migrate eastward and mix with the locals. Obvious "hybrids" are seen in winter and areas along the North Platte River in western Nebraska is where the zone of hybridization occurs. Northern Flickers are common throughout the year and are found in nearly every wooded area, be it shelterbelts or

Red-Headed Woodpecker
& bush clover   ©1994 Wm. S. Whitney

riparian forests. They wander some distance from trees to forage in grasslands, more so than other species of woodpeckers.

WILLOW FLYCATCHER and BELL'S VIREO- These two species are listed together because they share similar characteristics. Both species winter in the neotropics and occur here from April through September. Willow Flycatchers and Bell's Vireos nest in the riparian shrub zones of the Platte. They are uncommon due to the ephemeral nature of their preferred habitat. Look for young stands of willow or indigobush. Once you find the habitat, you will find the birds. Upstream of the Hwy 44 bridge at Kearney (about 1 mile south of I-80 Exit #272) is a good place to find them. Bader Park, Mormon Island Crane Meadows, Audubon's Rowe Sanctuary, and the Hike Bike Trail at Ft. Kearny State Historical Park also host nesting birds. They are more easily heard than seen although they respond well to "pishing." Western and southwestern populations of both species are declining rapidly, particularly along the riparian areas, where they are candidates for federal listing as endangered species.

EASTERN AND WESTERN KINGBIRD- Whether you are coming here from the east or the west, you will find a kingbird to your liking. Both species nest here and are common. The Western Kingbird is more cosmopolitan and can be found in open parks such as baseball fields in almost every town. I've found a number of Western Kingbird nests in isolated pines. The Eastern Kingbird is more at home along the open edges of riparian areas and has an affinity to nest over water. If you canoe the Platte during the summer (during those rare years when there is enough water to canoe), you are almost certain to find a nest in a sweeper (a tree that has partially fallen into the river). In September, Eastern Kingbirds begin to congregate in flocks of hundreds prior to migration. At that time, collisions with vehicles take a heavy toll on the birds as they dart out over the roads catching insects.

CLIFF SWALLOW- Many of the larger bridges crossing the Platte River host large colonies of Cliff Swallows. Hundreds of nests may be present at the largest sites. Their globular mud nests are unmistakable and swarms of swallows can hardly go unnoticed by even the most casual observer. Cliff Swallows are present from April through September.

BLACK-BILLED MAGPIE- Magpies reach their eastern limit here as a regular nesting species. They seem to have an affinity for Russian olives or red cedars as a nest site. Their large, domed nest is woven from twigs and branches sporting lots of thorns. Nesting occurs from April through June. The entrance hole is just large enough for the adults to squeeze through and is usually pointed away from the main supporting branch, a habit that is likely a response to discourage predation by bullsnakes. Isolated nests exist, although often there are several nests within a relatively small area. An individual nest may be used for several years, gradually being enlarged and reaching diameters of up to three feet. Magpies are found throughout the area where there are grasslands with scattered trees, except they avoid urban settings. In winter, they form loose groups and travel about scavenging roadkills or any other carcass they encounter. Unlike their rather tame cousins living in the mountains, these birds are shy and avoid human contact as much as possible.

SEDGE WREN- This peculiar wren inhabits the sedge meadows of the Platte River. They are highly localized with Mormon Island Crane Meadows being the best place to find them. Listen for singing males in late July and early August when they arrive to nest. They are often still incubating in September and are usually overlooked during Breeding Bird Surveys which take

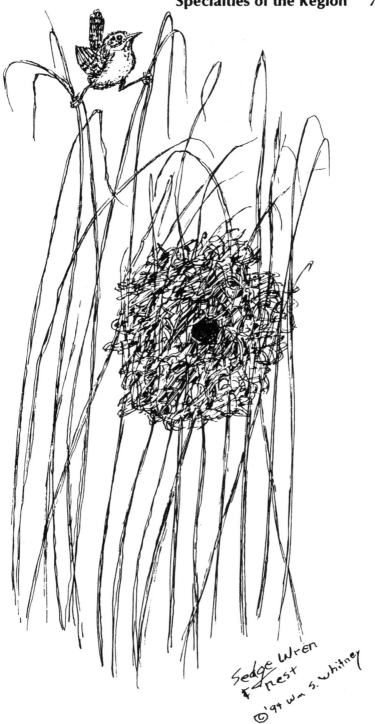

Sedge Wren
& nest
©'94 Wm S. Whitney

place in June, well before this species arrives in some years. Mouse-like in its habits, Sedge Wrens prefer to drop to the ground and scurry away in the dense vegetation rather than fly. Their globular nests are woven in sedges and contain up to 6 pearl-like eggs. Several dummy nests are built by the male who defends his territory while trying to attract a mate. It is the female that chooses the brood nest which can be distinguished from dummy nests by the lining of feathers. Whether this late nesting is a second effort by birds that nested in more northerly portions of their range remains a mystery. It is good to have mysteries and this unique little wren is of special interest to me because of that.

EASTERN BLUEBIRD- Bluebird box trails have sprung up all over the country, and this area is no exception. Their popularity may be explained by the willingness of bluebirds to use nest boxes. Constructing boxes and establishing a trail is a great project for local youth or conservation groups. The Nebraska Game and Parks Commission sponsors a Bluebird Trail Directory and has plans for building boxes. For more information contact their Lincoln office. Eastern Bluebirds begin searching for nest sites in March. They may have up to 3 or even 4 broods per nesting season. There are several trails in the area; Mormon Island Crane Meadows, Audubon's Rowe Sanctuary, Crane Meadows Nature Center, and Shoemaker Island are a few areas with trails. Bluebirds are found here throughout the year, although they are uncommon to rare in January and February. Competition for the boxes with House Sparrows is generally not a problem but House Wrens do compete for the boxes, especially if they are near brushy areas.

Bluebirds
©94 Wm. S. Whitney

LOGGERHEAD SHRIKE- This is another species whose story is one of a population in serious decline throughout most its range. Yet, if your only experience with Loggerhead Shrikes was in the Sandhills of Nebraska, you would undoubtedly be surprised at the concern given to this species in other states. Shrikes are a fairly common nesting species throughout the Sandhills although they are uncommon in this area as a nester. Egg dates in this area are from 3 May to 16 June. Brushy fencelines are where they nest here. Treetops, utility lines/poles, or the tops of corn stubble are commonly used perches. They occur here throughout the winter although they are most common during the fall migration (especially October) when more northerly populations pass through.

DICKCISSEL- This is the third member of a guild of grassland nesting species that share both their summer range here and their winter range in South America. The other two species are

Dickcissel
© '94 Wm. S. Whitney

Upland Sandpiper and Bobolink. Dickcissels are locally common and arrive in mid-May, 5 to 7 days later than Bobolinks. They linger in the area though early October. Dickcissels prefer to nest in alfalfa fields, a habit which makes their first nesting effort nearly impossible since the crop is harvested in early June, well before the nestlings have fledged. They will renest in adjacent areas, often in pastures which have adequate residual cover and stature. On Mormon Island Crane Meadows, egg dates range from 23 June through 8 August. They also congregate in larger flocks prior to fall migration.

GRASSHOPPER SPARROW- Present here from April through October, Grasshopper Sparrows winter in the neotropics. Populations appear to be declining throughout their range with

Grasshopper Sparrow
©94 Wm. S. Whitney

the exception of Nebraska in general (especially the Sandhills), and the Platte River meadows and bordering upland prairie in particular, where populations are stable. Their insect-like trill is barely audible to persons with good hearing and their ventriloquist qualities make them even more difficult to locate by sound. Look and listen for them in just about any prairie pasture from the hills of the Taylor Ranch to the wet meadows of the Platte. Just about all of the stubby-tailed, sparrow-like birds you encounter in open prairie will be this species. The males sing from prominent perches such as verbena stalks or barbed wire fences but are not always easy to locate. The nests are even more difficult to find. Active nests occur from 6 June to 24 July. Of the six nests I've examined, four (66%) have been parasitized by Brown-headed Cowbirds.

HARRIS' SPARROW- This is a much sought-after species by birders. It is a bird of the continental interior, wintering primarily in the central to southern Plains States and migrating north to their nesting grounds which extend from Churchill to the Mackenzie River delta. It is found from October through May in this area. Look for it in brushy habitats along roadsides or abandoned farmsteads. They are not commonly found in urban areas but will readily come to bird feeders in more open locations. The Crane Meadows Nature Center is a good place to find this species. It is most abundant in October and again in April as the wave of migrants pass through the area. Their whistle-like call has a similar tone to that of a White-crowned Sparrow which often accompany flocks of Harris' Sparrows. Look closely at groups of wintering American Tree Sparrows and Dark-eyed Juncos and you will often find a Harris' Sparrow among them.

BOBOLINK- First arrivals at Mormon Island Crane Meadows range from 2-11 May. Bobolinks are common nesters in suitable lowland prairie/wet meadow habitat. Like Upland Sandpipers, they depart from the area by late August. The males arrive in full nuptial regalia, defending territories with elaborate song flights. By late July, males take on the appearance of the comparatively drab females and fledglings. They become more sociable at this time of the year and form flocks of 40 individuals prior to migration. Walking through a wet meadow in June is a sensory delight. Bobolinks will no doubt accompany you as you intrude upon their territory. Their bubbling song mixed in with the songs of Upland Sandpipers and Western Meadowlarks soothes the ear. Add to that the splash of the delicate colors of prairie forbs such as blazing star, blue-eyed grass, and evening primrose and rich greens of the foliage, and you may experience the beauty of the prairie which captivated the famous Nebraska author, Willa Cather.

Bobolink
© '94 Wm. S. Whitney

EASTERN and WESTERN MEADOWLARK- The Western Meadowlark was designated as the official state bird in 1929. Seventy years later an effort to dethrone this species in favor of the Sandhill Crane was unsuccessful. Over 99% of the meadowlarks in this area are Western Meadowlarks. All wintering birds are presumed to be Western based on call notes. Birds nesting in the drier upland areas are Westerns as well. The Eastern Meadowlark is known to nest only on certain wet meadows bordering the Platte although it undoubtedly occurs elsewhere in lowland prairie habitat. The song is the only reliable way for most birders to distinguish the two species in the field.

Meadowlark
@99 wm. s. whiney

YELLOW-HEADED BLACKBIRD- Large flocks of migrants begin to show in April and they can be seen virtually in any open area. Yellow-headed Blackbirds have nested at Deep Well WPA, Funk Lagoon, I-80 mm #287-288 and #289-290 on the north side, or any area that supports extensive stands of cattails or bulrush. Their rather rank call belies their striking plumage. This species is considered a nuisance in the late summer and fall when huge flocks depredate crops such as sunflower or wheat, a problem most pronounced in North Dakota.

GREAT-TAILED GRACKLE- This species has expanded its range and is now near its northern limit here. It was first recorded in this area as a nesting species in 1976. There are several sites where Great-tailed Grackles nest beginning in early May. Grackles remain near their nesting sites through August. They nest in the cattails at Funk Lagoon and in a cattail marsh on the north side of I-80 between mm #287-288 and #289-290. These noisy birds also nest in red cedar shelterbelts. In Grand Island, head 7 miles north on Highway 281 from I-80 Exit #312 to Old Potash Hwy, turn left (west) and search any red cedar belts you encounter within a 1/2 mile radius. Great-tailed Grackles have nested in this general area for the last 14 years. In Adams County, red cedar belts 1.5- 3 miles east of Hastings Highway 6 by-pass in the vicinity of Central Community College and the U.S. Ammunitions Depot have hosted nesting grackles for the past several years as well.

NORTHERN ORIOLE- Like the flicker, we lost the "Baltimore" and "Bullock's" oriole in 1983 when they were lumped as the Northern Oriole. Rumor has it that they will likely be split once again when the American Ornithologist's Union releases the next nomenclature revision due out in 1994, so beware. At any rate, the "Baltimore" variety is the one found in this area; however, "Bullock's" occur southwest of North Platte. Orioles are found both in town and in the country where they nest in mature trees. Their melodious song brightens any day, not to mention their stunning color. This species is fairly common and their pendulant nests are very conspicuous after the leaves have dropped. High winds can wreak havoc on eggs and nestlings as they are tossed from their nests, yet populations seem to be stable in this area.

HOUSE FINCH- This species is a newcomer here, having first been recorded nesting in Grand Island in April 1983. They have become well-established and have displaced House Sparrows to some extent, which is a welcome change. Whether these birds pioneered here from the East or West is unclear but the best guess is from the West. They are almost exclusively an urban dweller and have a preference to nest in spruce or pine trees. House Finches readily take to feeders in the winter, especially if black oil sunflower seeds or Niger thistle seeds are provided. They have been a regular addition to the Grand Island Christmas Bird Count nearly every year since 1981.

©'94 wm.S.whimey

BIRDS OF THE PLATTE

The following species list is the heart and soul of this guide. It is based largely on my own observations and sightings reported to me or published in the *Nebraska Bird Review* from 1978 through 1994. About 75% of the species found in Nebraska occur here. Over half of the 300 species listed are neotropical migrants; species with populations that winter largely south of the Tropic of Cancer but nest north of the tropics. Recent declines in this group of birds has focused much attention on conservation efforts in North America and Latin America. A total of 115 species nest in this area. We often think of spring and fall as the period for bird migration, but migration through Nebraska occurs in every month of the year, although January can be slow at times.

The "Observability" code is a subjective ranking of your chances of seeing a particular species. The following key explains what each number means:

> 1= Easy
> 2= Probably
> 3= Maybe
> 4= Unlikely
> 5= Congratulations

This ranking assumes that you are searching the proper habitat at the right time of the year. Perhaps you will be lucky enough to spot a new month for a certain species or, better yet, you may discover an entirely new species. I would appreciate receiving your observations so that they may be incorporated into future editions of this guide. Any rare sightings should be carefully documented and sent to the Records Committee of the Nebraska Ornithologists' Union (see Sighting Report Form).

☑	Ja	Fe	Mr	Ap	My	Jn	Jl	Au	Se	Oc	No	De	N†	O*
☐ Common Loon				♦	♦	♦	♦	♦			*			3
☐ Pied-billed Grebe††			♦	♦	♦	♦	♦	♦	♦	♦	♦		N	1
☐ Horned Grebe			♦		♦									3
☐ Eared Grebe				♦	♦	♦	♦	♦		♦			N	2
☐ Western Grebe					♦			♦	♦				N	4
☐ American White Pelican				♦	♦	♦	♦	♦	♦	♦	♦	♦	N	1
☐ Double-crested Cormorant			♦	♦	♦	♦	♦	♦	♦	♦	♦	♦		1
☐ American Bittern				♦	♦		♦	♦	♦					3
☐ Least Bittern					♦			♦					N	4
☐ Great Blue Heron	♦	♦	♦	♦	♦	♦	♦	♦	♦	♦	♦	♦	N	1
☐ Great Egret				♦	♦	♦	♦	♦	♦	♦			N	2
☐ Snowy Egret				♦	♦	♦	♦	♦	♦				N	3
☐ Little Blue Heron				♦	♦		♦	♦	♦	♦			N	3
☐ Cattle Egret				♦	♦	♦		♦	♦	♦			N	2
☐ Green Heron				♦	♦	♦	♦	♦	♦	♦			N	1
☐ Black-crowned Night-Heron				♦	♦		♦	♦	♦	♦				2
☐ Yellow-crowned Night-Heron					♦		♦	♦					N	5
☐ White-faced Ibis				♦	♦	♦		♦	♦	♦	♦		N	3
☐ Tundra Swan		♦	♦											4
☐ Trumpeter Swan	♦	♦	♦								♦	♦		5
☐ Mute Swan	♦	♦	♦	♦	♦	♦	♦	♦	♦	♦	♦	♦		4
☐ Greater White-fronted Goose	♦	♦	♦	♦	♦	♦		♦	♦	♦	♦	♦	N	1
☐ Snow Goose	♦	♦	♦	♦	♦		♦	♦	♦	♦	♦	♦		1
☐ Ross' Goose			♦	♦	♦	♦								2
☐ Brant			♦											5
☐ Canada Goose	♦	♦	♦	♦	♦	♦	♦	♦	♦	♦	♦	♦		1
☐ Wood Duck	♦	♦	♦	♦	♦	♦	♦	♦	♦	♦	♦	♦		1
☐ Green-winged Teal		♦	♦	♦	♦	♦	♦	♦	♦	♦	♦	♦		1

☑		Ja	Fe	Mr	Ap	My	Jn	Jl	Au	Se	Oc	No	De	N'	O*
☐	American Black Duck	◆	◆										◆		4
☐	Mallard	◆	◆	◆	◆	◆	◆	◆	◆	◆	◆	◆	◆		1
☐	Northern Pintail	◆	◆	◆	◆	◆	◆	◆	◆	◆	◆	◆	◆	N	1
☐	Blue-winged Teal				◆	◆	◆	◆	◆	◆	◆			N	1
☐	Cinnamon Teal				◆	◆	◆							N	2
☐	Northern Shoveler				◆	◆	◆	◆	◆	◆	◆	◆	◆	N	1
☐	Gadwall	◆	◆	◆	◆	◆	◆	◆	◆	◆	◆	◆	◆		1
☐	Eurasian Wigeon				◆	◆									5
☐	American Wigeon	◆	◆	◆	◆	◆	◆	◆	◆	◆	◆	◆	◆	N	1
☐	Canvasback	◆	◆	◆	◆	◆					◆	◆	◆		2
☐	Redhead		◆	◆	◆	◆	◆			◆	◆	◆	◆	N	1
☐	Ring-necked Duck		◆	◆	◆	◆				◆	◆	◆	◆	N	1
☐	Greater Scaup			◆	◆										3
☐	Lesser Scaup	◆	◆	◆	◆	◆				◆	◆	◆	◆	N	1
☐	Surf Scoter				◆										5
☐	White-winged Scoter										◆				5
☐	Common Goldeneye	◆	◆	◆	◆						◆	◆	◆		4
☐	Bufflehead		◆	◆	◆	◆					◆	◆	◆		1
☐	Hooded Merganser	◆	◆	◆			◆		◆		◆	◆	◆		3
☐	Common Merganser	◆	◆	◆	◆	◆	◆	◆		◆	◆	◆	◆		1
☐	Red-breasted Merganser		◆	◆	◆	◆									3
☐	Ruddy Duck	◆		◆	◆	◆	◆	◆	◆	◆	◆	◆		N	1
☐	Turkey Vulture			◆	◆	◆	◆	◆	◆	◆	◆		◆	N	2
☐	Osprey				◆	◆	◆		◆	◆	◆		◆	N	2
☐	White-tailed Kite							◆	◆	◆					5
☐	Mississippi Kite						◆	◆	◆	◆				N	3
☐	Bald Eagle	◆	◆	◆	◆	◆	◆	◆	◆	◆	◆	◆	◆		1
☐	Northern Harrier	◆	◆	◆	◆	◆			◆	◆	◆	◆	◆	N	1

☑	Ja	Fe	Mr	Ap	My	Jn	Jl	Au	Se	Oc	No	De	N†	O*
☐ Sharp-shinned Hawk	•	•	•	•	•			•	•	•	•	•	N	2
☐ Cooper's Hawk	•	•	•	•				•	•	•	•	•	N	3
☐ Northern Goshawk	•		•	•				•	•	•	•			4
☐ Broad-winged Hawk				•	•			•					N	5
☐ Swainson's Hawk				•	•	•	•	•	•				N	1
☐ Red-tailed Hawk	•	•	•	•	•	•	•	•	•	•	•	•		1
☐ Ferruginous Hawk	•	•	•		•				•	•	•	•		2
☐ Rough-legged Hawk	•	•	•	•					•	•	•	•		1
☐ Golden Eagle	•	•	•	•	•				•	•	•			3
☐ American Kestrel	•	•	•	•	•	•	•	•	•	•	•	•		1
☐ Merlin	•	•	•	•						•	•	N	3
☐ Peregrine Falcon		•	•	•	•			•		•		•	N	3
☐ Prairie Falcon	•	•	•						•	•	•	•	N	2
☐ Ring-necked Pheasant	•	•	•	•	•	•	•	•	•	•	•	•		1
☐ Greater Prairie-Chicken	•	•	•	•	•	•	•	•	•	•	•	•		1
☐ Sharp-tailed Grouse	•	•	•	•	•	•	•	•	•	•	•	•		2
☐ Wild Turkey	•	•	•	•	•	•	•	•	•	•	•	•		1
☐ Northern Bobwhite	•	•	•	•	•	•	•	•	•	•	•	•		1
☐ Yellow Rail								•						5
☐ Black Rail					•									5
☐ King Rail						•								5
☐ Virginia Rail				•	•	•	•	•	•					3
☐ Sora				•	•	•		•	•	•			N	2
☐ American Coot	•	•	•	•	•	•	•	•	•	•	•	•		1
☐ Sandhill Crane	•	•	•	•	•	•	•		•	•	•	•		1
☐ Whooping Crane			•	•					•	•	•			4
☐ Black-bellied Plover					•	•		•	•	•			N	3
☐ American Golden-Plover			•	•	•	•	•		•				N	3

☑	Ja	Fe	Mr	Ap	My	Jn	Jl	Au	Se	Oc	No	De	N†	O*
☐ Snowy Plover					•		•						N	4
☐ Semipalmated Plover				•	•	•	•	•	•				N	2
☐ Piping Plover				•	•	•	•	•						1
☐ Killdeer	•	•	•	•	•	•	•	•	•	•	•	•		1
☐ Mountain Plover					•								N	5
☐ Black-necked Stilt					•								N	5
☐ American Avocet				•	•	•	•	•	•	•			N	2
☐ Greater Yellowlegs			•	•	•	•	•	•	•	•	•		N	1
☐ Lesser Yellowlegs			•	•	•		•	•	•	•			N	1
☐ Solitary Sandpiper				•	•		•	•					N	2
☐ Willet				•	•		•	•					N	2
☐ Spotted Sandpiper				•	•	•	•	•	•				N	1
☐ Upland Sandpiper				•	•	•	•	•					N	1
☐ Eskimo Curlew				•	•								N	5
☐ Whimbrel					•		•						N	5
☐ Long-billed Curlew				•	•								N	5
☐ Hudsonian Godwit				•	•								N	3
☐ Marbled Godwit				•	•			•					N	3
☐ Red Knot					•								N	5
☐ Ruddy Turnstone					•		•						N	4
☐ Sanderling				•	•	•			•				N	3
☐ Semipalmated Sandpiper			•	•	•		•	•	•				N	1
☐ Western Sandpiper					•		•	•	•	•			N	3
☐ Least Sandpiper	•			•	•		•	•	•	•			N	1
☐ White-rumped Sandpiper					•	•	•	•	•				N	1
☐ Baird's Sandpiper			•	•	•	•	•	•	•				N	1
☐ Pectoral Sandpiper				•	•	•	•	•	•	•			N	1
☐ Dunlin				•	•									3

☑	Ja	Fe	Mr	Ap	My	Jn	Jl	Au	Se	Oc	No	De	N†	O*
Stilt Sandpiper					♦	♦	♦	♦					N	2
Buff-breasted Sandpiper				♦	♦			♦					N	3
Short-billed Dowitcher					♦				♦	♦			N	4
Long-billed Dowitcher			♦	♦	♦		♦	♦	♦	♦			N	2
Common Snipe	♦	♦	♦	♦	♦	♦	♦	♦	♦	♦	♦	♦	N	1
American Woodcock			♦	♦	♦	♦	♦	♦	♦	♦				1
Wilson's Phalarope				♦	♦	♦	♦	♦	♦				N	1
Red-necked Phalarope					♦			♦	♦				N	3
Red Phalarope								♦	♦				N	5
Franklin's Gull			♦	♦	♦	♦		♦	♦	♦			N	1
Bonaparte's Gull				♦	♦								N	3
Ring-billed Gull		♦	♦	♦	♦	♦	♦	♦	♦	♦	♦	♦	N	1
Herring Gull		♦	♦	♦	♦			♦		♦				4
Caspian Tern					♦	♦	♦	♦	♦				N	4
Common Tern				♦									N	4
Forster's Tern					♦	♦	♦	♦	♦	♦			N	1
Least Tern					♦	♦	♦	♦	♦	♦			N	1
Black Tern					♦	♦	♦	♦	♦				N	1
Rock Dove	♦	♦	♦	♦	♦	♦	♦	♦	♦	♦	♦	♦		1
Mourning Dove	♦	♦	♦	♦	♦	♦	♦	♦	♦	♦	♦	♦		1
Inca Dove	♦									♦	♦	♦		5
Black-billed Cuckoo					♦	♦	♦	♦	♦				N	2
Yellow-billed Cuckoo					♦	♦	♦	♦	♦				N	2
Barn Owl	♦	♦	♦	♦	♦	♦	♦	♦	♦	♦	♦	♦		3
Eastern Screech-Owl	♦	♦	♦	♦	♦	♦	♦	♦	♦	♦	♦	♦		1
Great Horned Owl	♦	♦	♦	♦	♦	♦	♦	♦	♦	♦	♦	♦		1
Snowy Owl											♦	♦		4
Burrowing Owl				♦	♦	♦	♦	♦	♦	♦				2

☑		Ja	Fe	Mr	Ap	My	Jn	Jl	Au	Se	Oc	No	De	N†	O*
☐	Barred Owl						◆								4
☐	Long-eared Owl											◆			4
☐	Short-eared Owl	◆	◆	◆							◆	◆	◆		2
☐	Northern Saw-whet Owl		◆												5
☐	Common Nighthawk					◆	◆	◆	◆	◆	◆			N	1
☐	Common Poorwill									◆	◆			N	5
☐	Chuck-will's Widow						◆							N	5
☐	Chimney Swift				◆	◆	◆	◆	◆	◆				N	1
☐	Ruby-throated Hummingbird					◆		◆	◆	◆				N	3
☐	Broad-tailed Hummingbird									◆				N	5
☐	Rufous Hummingbird									◆				N	5
☐	Belted Kingfisher	◆	◆	◆	◆	◆	◆	◆	◆	◆	◆	◆	◆	N	1
☐	Red-headed Woodpecker		◆		◆	◆	◆	◆	◆	◆	◆	◆	◆		1
☐	Red-bellied Woodpecker	◆	◆	◆	◆	◆	◆	◆	◆	◆	◆	◆	◆		2
☐	Yellow-bellied Sapsucker		◆	◆	◆	◆					◆	◆	◆	N	3
☐	Downy Woodpecker	◆	◆	◆	◆	◆	◆	◆	◆	◆	◆	◆	◆		1
☐	Hairy Woodpecker	◆	◆	◆	◆	◆	◆	◆	◆	◆	◆	◆	◆		2
☐	Northern Flicker	◆	◆	◆	◆	◆	◆	◆	◆	◆	◆	◆	◆		1
☐	Olive-sided Flycatcher					◆								N	4
☐	Eastern Wood-Pewee					◆	◆	◆	◆	◆	◆			N	2
☐	Yellow-bellied Flycatcher					◆								N	4
☐	Willow Flycatcher				◆	◆	◆	◆	◆	◆				N	1
☐	Least Flycatcher					◆					◆			N	2
☐	Eastern Phoebe				◆	◆			◆	◆	◆	◆		N	2
☐	Say's Phoebe			◆	◆			◆	◆	◆				N	3
☐	Great Crested Flycatcher					◆	◆	◆	◆					N	1
☐	Western Kingbird					◆	◆	◆	◆	◆				N	1
☐	Eastern Kingbird					◆	◆	◆	◆	◆				N	1

☑		Ja	Fe	Mr	Ap	My	Jn	Jl	Au	Se	Oc	No	De	N'	O*
☐	Horned Lark	•	•	•	•	•	•	•			•	•	•		1
☐	Purple Martin				•	•	•	•	•	•				N	1
☐	Tree Swallow				•	•	•	•	•	•				N	1
☐	Violet-green Swallow							•						N	1
☐	N. Rough-winged Swallow				•	•	•	•	•	•				N	1
☐	Bank Swallow				•	•	•	•	•	•				N	1
☐	Cliff Swallow				•	•	•	•	•	•				N	1
☐	Barn Swallow				•	•	•	•	•	•	•			N	1
☐	Blue Jay	•	•	•	•	•	•	•	•	•	•	•	•		1
☐	Clark's Nutcracker											•			5
☐	Black-billed Magpie	•	•	•	•	•	•	•	•	•	•	•	•		2
☐	American Crow	•	•	•	•	•	•	•	•	•	•	•	•		1
☐	Black-capped Chickadee	•	•	•	•	•	•	•	•	•	•	•	•		1
☐	Tufted Titmouse				•	•									4
☐	Red-breasted Nuthatch	•	•	•	•	•					•	•			2
☐	White-breasted Nuthatch	•	•	•	•	•	•	•	•	•	•	•	•		1
☐	Brown Creeper	•	•	•	•	•					•	•	•		3
☐	Rock Wren										•				5
☐	Carolina Wren			•							•		•		4
☐	Bewick's Wren				•	•									4
☐	House Wren				•	•	•	•	•	•	•				1
☐	Winter Wren				•										4
☐	Sedge Wren					•	•	•	•	•	•				1
☐	Marsh Wren				•	•		•	•	•	•				2
☐	Golden-crowned Kinglet	•	•	•	•						•	•	•		2
☐	Ruby-crowned Kinglet	•			•	•				•	•	•	•	N	2
☐	Eastern Bluebird	•	•	•	•	•	•	•	•	•	•	•	•		1
☐	Mountain Bluebird	•	•										•		3

☑		Ja	Fe	Mr	Ap	My	Jn	Jl	Au	Se	Oc	No	De	N'	O*
☐	Townsend's Solitaire		♦	♦							♦	♦	♦		3
☐	Veery					♦								N	3
☐	Gray-cheeked Thrush					♦								N	3
☐	Swainson's Thrush					♦				♦				N	2
☐	Hermit Thrush					♦					♦			N	4
☐	American Robin	♦	♦	♦	♦	♦	♦	♦	♦	♦	♦	♦	♦		1
☐	Gray Catbird					♦	♦	♦	♦	♦	♦		♦	N	2
☐	Northern Mockingbird					♦	♦		♦				♦		4
☐	Brown Thrasher			♦	♦	♦	♦	♦	♦	♦	♦	♦	♦	N	1
☐	American Pipit			♦	♦					♦	♦			N	3
☐	Sprague's Pipit				♦	♦					♦			N	3
☐	Bohemian Waxwing	♦													4
☐	Cedar Waxwing	♦	♦	♦	♦	♦	♦	♦	♦	♦	♦	♦	♦		2
☐	Northern Shrike	♦	♦	♦							♦	♦	♦		3
☐	Loggerhead Shrike	♦		♦	♦	♦	♦	♦	♦	♦		♦	♦		2
☐	European Starling	♦	♦	♦	♦	♦	♦	♦	♦	♦	♦	♦	♦		1
☐	Bell's Vireo				♦	♦	♦	♦	♦	♦				N	1
☐	Solitary Vireo					♦								N	3
☐	Yellow-throated Vireo					♦								N	4
☐	Warbling Vireo				♦	♦	♦	♦	♦	♦				N	1
☐	Philadelphia Vireo					♦							♦	N	3
☐	Red-eyed Vireo				♦	♦	♦							N	4
☐	Blue-winged Warbler					♦								N	5
☐	Golden-winged Warbler					♦								N	5
☐	Tennessee Warbler					♦								N	2
☐	Orange-crowned Warbler				♦	♦				♦	♦			N	1
☐	Nashville Warbler					♦				♦	♦			N	3
☐	Yellow Warbler					♦	♦	♦	♦	♦				N	1

☑	Ja	Fe	Mr	Ap	My	Jn	Jl	Au	Se	Oc	No	De	N†	O*
☐ Chestnut-sided Warbler					◆								N	2
☐ Magnolia Warbler					◆								N	3
☐ Cape May Warbler					◆								N	4
☐ Black-throated Blue Warbler					◆								N	4
☐ Yellow-rumped Warbler				◆	◆				◆	◆				1
☐ Black-throated Green Warbler					◆	◆				◆			N	4
☐ Blackburnian Warbler					◆								N	3
☐ Yellow-throated Warbler					◆								N	4
☐ Palm Warbler					◆								N	3
☐ Bay-breasted Warbler					◆								N	4
☐ Blackpoll Warbler					◆								N	2
☐ Black-and-white Warbler					◆								N	2
☐ American Redstart					◆			◆					N	2
☐ Ovenbird					◆	◆		◆					N	3
☐ Northern Waterthrush					◆								N	3
☐ Louisiana Waterthrush					◆								N	4
☐ Kentucky Warbler					◆								N	4
☐ Mourning Warbler					◆				◆				N	4
☐ Common Yellowthroat				◆	◆	◆	◆	◆	◆				N	1
☐ Wilson's Warbler					◆			◆	◆	◆			N	3
☐ Yellow-breasted Chat					◆								N	4
☐ Summer Tanager				◆									N	5
☐ Scarlet Tanager						◆							N	5
☐ Northern Cardinal	◆	◆	◆	◆	◆	◆	◆	◆	◆	◆	◆	◆		1
☐ Rose-breasted Grosbeak				◆	◆	◆	◆	◆	◆				N	2
☐ Black-headed Grosbeak				◆	◆	◆	◆						N	3
☐ Blue Grosbeak					◆	◆	◆	◆					N	2
☐ Lazuli Bunting					◆								N	4

☑	Ja	Fe	Mr	Ap	My	Jn	Jl	Au	Se	Oc	No	De	N†	O*
☒ Painted Bunting											•		N	5
☐ Indigo Bunting					•	•	•	•					N	2
☒ Dickcissel					•	•	•	•	•	•			N	1
☐ Rufous-sided Towhee	•	•		•	•	•	•	•	•	•	•	•		1
☒ American Tree Sparrow	•	•	•	•	•					•	•	•		1
☐ Chipping Sparrow				•	•	•	•	•	•	•	•	•		1
☒ Clay-colored Sparrow					•	•			•	•			N	1
☐ Field Sparrow		•		•	•	•	•	•	•	•		•		1
☒ Vesper Sparrow	•		•	•	•				•	•	•	•		1
☐ Lark Sparrow				•	•	•	•	•	•	•			N	1
☒ Lark Bunting					•	•	•	•						3
☐ Savannah Sparrow			•	•	•				•	•	•			1
☒ Grasshopper Sparrow				•	•	•	•	•	•	•	•		N	1
☐ Henslow's Sparrow					•				•					5
☒ Le Conte's Sparrow				•	•				•	•	•			4
☐ Sharp-tailed Sparrow		•			•					•				4
☒ Fox Sparrow				•	•						•			4
☐ Song Sparrow	•	•	•	•	•	•	•	•	•	•	•	•		1
☒ Lincoln's Sparrow			•	•	•				•	•		•	N	2
☐ Swamp Sparrow	•			•	•				•	•				3
☒ White-throated Sparrow				•	•				•	•	•	•		2
☐ White-crowned Sparrow	•	•		•	•	•			•	•	•	•		2
☒ Harris' Sparrow	•	•	•	•	•					•	•	•		1
☐ Dark-eyed Junco	•	•	•	•	•				•	•	•	•		1
☒ Lapland Longspur	•		•							•	•	•		3
☐ Bobolink					•	•	•	•	•				N	1
☒ Red-winged Blackbird	•	•	•	•	•	•	•	•	•	•	•	•		1
☐ Eastern Meadowlark			•	•	•	•	•							2

☑	Ja	Fe	Mr	Ap	My	Jn	Jl	Au	Se	Oc	No	De	N†	O*
☐ **Western Meadowlark**	◆	◆	◆	◆	◆	◆	◆	◆	◆	◆	◆	◆		1
☐ Yellow-headed Blackbird			◆	◆	◆	◆	◆	◆	◆	◆	◆		N	1
☐ **Rusty Blackbird**		◆	◆							◆	◆	◆		3
☐ Brewer's Blackbird	◆				◆			◆	◆	◆	◆			3
☐ **Great-tailed Grackle**	◆	◆	◆	◆	◆	◆	◆	◆	◆	◆	◆	◆		1
☐ Common Grackle	◆	◆	◆	◆	◆	◆	◆	◆	◆	◆	◆	◆		1
☐ **Brown-headed Cowbird**			◆	◆	◆	◆	◆	◆	◆	◆		◆		1
☐ Orchard Oriole					◆	◆	◆	◆					N	1
☐ **Northern Oriole**					◆	◆	◆	◆	◆				N	1
☐ Gray-crowned Rosy-Finch											◆			5
☐ **Pine Grosbeak**												◆		5
☐ Purple Finch	◆										◆	◆		3
☐ **House Finch**	◆	◆	◆	◆	◆	◆	◆	◆	◆	◆	◆	◆		1
☐ Red Crossbill	◆	◆	◆	◆								◆		3
☐ **White-winged Crossbill**	◆													5
☐ Common Redpoll	◆			◆										4
☐ **Pine Siskin**	◆	◆	◆	◆	◆				◆	◆	◆	◆		1
☐ American Goldfinch	◆	◆	◆	◆	◆	◆	◆	◆	◆	◆	◆	◆		1
☐ **Evening Grosbeak**	◆	◆	◆	◆							◆	◆		4
☐ House Sparrow	◆	◆	◆	◆	◆	◆	◆	◆	◆	◆	◆	◆		1
TOTAL SPECIES =	94	95	125	190	243	148	145	164	166	160	118	114	164	300

† N= neotropical migrant; a species that winters south of the Tropic of Cancer and nests
   north of this line.
†† **Boldface** indicates a species that nests in the area.
* O= Observability Code: 1= Easy
                            2= Probably
                            3= Maybe
                            4= Unlikely
                            5= Congratulations
Names according to American Ornithologists' Union. 1993. Thirty-ninth supplement to
the A.O.U. *Checklist of North American Birds*. Auk 110:675-682 and previous revisions.

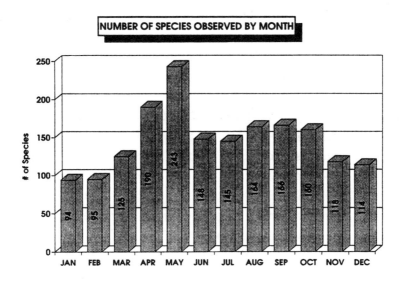

NUMBER OF SPECIES OBSERVED BY MONTH

# of Species

JAN	FEB	MAR	APR	MAY	JUN	JUL	AUG	SEP	OCT	NOV	DEC
94	95	125	190	243	148	145	164	166	160	116	114

LOCAL CONTACTS AND CONSERVATION ORGANIZATIONS

1) **NEBRASKA BIRD HOTLINE**: (402) 292-5325. Weekly tapes tell of the latest birding news.

2) **THE PLATTE RIVER WHOOPING CRANE MAINTENANCE TRUST**, 2550 N. Diers Ave., Suite H, Grand Island, NE 68803; (308) 384-4633; FAX: (308) 384-4634.

   The Trust manages over 9,000 acres of Platte River habitat for migratory birds. Permission is required for entry on their property. Their book *Migratory Bird Habitat on the Platte and North Platte Rivers, Nebraska* may be purchased for $11 postpaid. It describes how habitat for migratory birds has changed since European settlement and how species have adjusted to these changes. They also publish a newsletter called *The Braided River* which contains information on pertinent activities in the area. Subscriptions are free. Simply send a request to be placed on the mailing list. (See page 35).

3) **NATIONAL AUDUBON SOCIETY'S LILLIAN ANNETTE ROWE SANCTUARY**, Rt. 2, Box 146, Gibbon, NE 68840; (308) 468-5282.

   Known locally as the Rowe Sanctuary, this site comprises about 2,200 acres. Guided crane tours to blinds are available by reservation. Permission is required for entry on the property throughout the year. The Mark Bolin Nature Trail is open to the public. (See page 27).

4)   RAINWATER BASIN WETLAND DISTRICT, U.S. Fish & Wildlife Service, P.O. Box 1686, 2610 Ave. Q, Kearney, NE 68848; (308) 236-5015.

This office manages over 21,300 acres at 55 sites within the Rainwater Basin. County maps showing these areas and a checklist of the birds of the Rainwater Basin are available free for the asking. They also host tours to view waterfowl and Sandhill Cranes through March and early April on a reservation basis.

5)   FORT KEARNY STATE HISTORICAL PARK, RR 4, Kearney, NE 68847; (308) 234-9513.

This park has a visitors center which caters to crane-watchers in the spring. Several publications and general information are available there. They also have blinds available for photographers on a reservation basis and a Hike Bike Trail which offers crane-viewing opportunities and good birding in general. (See page 45).

6)   PRAIRIE PLAINS RESOURCE INSTITUTE, 1307 L St., Aurora, NE 68818-2126; (402) 694-5535.

This membership organization is committed to prairie awareness, protection, and public education. The Institute sponsors free guided Nature tours to Bader Memorial Park on the Platte River and have published an interpretive guide to the natural history of the area entitled *Microcosm of the Platte, a Guide to Bader Memorial Park Natural Area* available for $10 postpaid. They manage some small native prairies and are experts on prairie restoration. A week-long immersion in outdoor education called SOAR (Summer Orientation About Rivers) is sponsored by the Institute. This program is geared toward elementary-aged children and has limited enrollment.

7)   **CRANE MEADOWS NATURE CENTER**, 9775 S. Alda Rd,
Wood River, NE 68883; (308) 382-1820.

This membership organization utilizes 240 acres of
prime river habitat leased to them by the Platte River
Whooping Crane Trust. They have a number of nature
trails and offer interpretive programs. Guided tours to a
crane-viewing blind are offered on a reservation basis.
Their mission is to provide environmental education to
people of all ages. (See page 36).

8)   **THE NATURE CONSERVANCY**, Nebraska Chapter Field
Office, 1722 St. Mary's Ave, Suite 403, Omaha, NE 68102;
(402) 342-0282. Aurora Project Office: (402) 694-4191.

TNC is a national membership organization
committed to preserving biological diversity by protecting
natural lands and the life they harbor. They manage
nearly 2,000 acres of Platte River habitat specifically for
Sandhill Cranes and work closely with the U.S. Fish &
Wildlife Service in acquiring sites in the Rainwater Basin.
They also offer field trips to view cranes in the spring.

9)   **NEBRASKA GAME & PARKS COMMISSION**, P.O. Box
30370, Lincoln, NE 68503; (402) 471-0641. North Platte
Field Office, Rt. 4, Box 39, North Platte, NE 69101; (308)
535-8025.

This state agency has several informative
brochures available free of charge. For information on
public lands and state campgrounds in the area ask for
the following: "Nebraska State Parks," "Public Hunting
Lands," and "Your Wildlife Lands, the Platte Valley."
They also have information on viewing dancing prairie
grouse from blinds. The North Platte Office has
information regarding viewing Sandhill Cranes in the

Hershey area west of North Platte and on wintering Bald Eagle viewing at Lake McConaughy.

10)   The following organizations offer blinds on leks of Greater Prairie-Chickens and/or Sharp-tailed Grouse on a reservation basis from March through early May weather permitting.

Valentine NWR   Nebr. Game & Parks Comm.
HC 14, Box 67   P.O. Box 30370
Valentine, NE 69201   Lincoln, NE 68503
(402) 376-3789   (402) 471-0641

U.S. Forest Service
Bessey Ranger District
P.O. Box 38
Halsey, NE 69142
(308) 533-2257 *or*
McKelvie Ranger District
(402) 823-4154

11)   CENTRAL NEBRASKA PUBLIC POWER AND IRRIGATION DISTRICT, P.O. Box 740, Holdrege, NE 68949; (308) 995-8601.
        They offer Bald Eagle viewing at the J-2 Power Plant from December through February. During the coldest weather, Bald Eagles congregate along the warm-water discharge below the plant where they feed on fish. When the weather warms they can be found perched in trees along nearby reaches of the Platte River.

12)   **NEBRASKA PUBLIC POWER DISTRICT**, P.O. Box 499,
Columbus, NE 68602-8561; (402) 563-5329.

       NPPD manages some sites specifically for nesting
Least Terns and Piping Plovers. Visitors are welcomed on
a reservation basis. Contact NPPD for specific
information.

13)   **NEBRASKA ORNITHOLOGISTS' UNION**, W436 Nebraska
Hall, Univ. of Nebraska, Lincoln, NE 68588.

       This is the state ornithological society and is
among the oldest in the nation. NOU publishes a
quarterly journal *The Nebraska Bird Review* and a
bimonthly newsletter.

14)   **HASTINGS MUSEUM**, 1330 N. Burlington, Hastings, NE
68901; (402) 461-2399.

       The Hastings Museum has natural history
displays of many of the region's avifauna including a large
display of Whooping Cranes. An Imax theater is another
feature of this museum.

15)   **BUFFALO COUNTY CONVENTION AND VISITORS
BUREAU**, P.O. Box 607, Kearney, NE 68848; (800)
652-9435 or (308) 237-3101.

       For a free copy of the "Crane Watch" brochure and
information regarding the Audubon River Conference,
contact them. The "Crane Watch" brochure has a map of
the best roads for viewing cranes and other migratory
birds. They also have information on bus tours to view
cranes in March.

16)   HALL COUNTY CONVENTION AND VISITORS BUREAU, P.O.
Box 607, Grand Island, NE 68802; (800) 658-3178 or (308)
382-4400.

They have similar information as the Buffalo
County group except they deal with the Grand Island
area. They also have information on the "Wings Over the
Platte" celebration occurring each March which boasts an
art show, crane tours, free seminars, and a banquet.

17)   U.S. FISH & WILDLIFE SERVICE, 203 W. 2nd St.,
Grand Island, NE 68801; (308) 382-6468.

General information regarding public lands and
endangered species of Nebraska can be obtained here.

18)   BIG BEND AUDUBON SOCIETY, Ward Schrack,
President, RR 4, Kearney, NE 68847; (308) 237-7296.

This local chapter of the National Audubon Society
sponsors field trips and an annual Christmas Bird Count.

19)   GRAND ISLAND CHAPTER OF AUDUBON, Scott Purdy,
President, 2222 Bellwood Dr., Apt. 104, Grand Island, NE
68803; (308) 384-8903.

This local chapter of the National Audubon Society
sponsors field trips, bluebird trail, an annual Christmas
Bird Count, and a bird identification class. Publishes the
Platte River Journal, a periodical newsletter.

20)   WHOOPING CRANE CONSERVATION ASSOCIATION,
1007 Carmel Ave., Lafayette, LA 70501; (318) 234-6339.

A membership organization working to prevent
the extinction of the Whooping Crane and save wetland
habitats. Publishes a quarterly newsletter, *Grus
Americana*.

21)   North American Crane Working Group, 2550 N. Diers Ave., Suite H, Grand Island, NE 68803; (308) 384-4633.

A membership organization dedicated to the conservation of cranes and their habitat in North America. Publishes *The Unison Call*, a semi-annual newsletter, and sponsors crane workshops every 3-4 years.

22)   International Crane Foundation, P.O. Box 447, Baraboo, WI 53913-0447; (608) 356-9462.

A membership organization dedicated to the preservation of cranes worldwide through research, conservation, captive propagation, restocking, field ecology, and public education. Publishes the *ICF Bugle*.

23)   Stuhr Museum of the Prairie Pioneer, 3133 W. Hwy 34, Grand Island, NE 68801; (308) 381-5316.

The Stuhr Museum's theme dates in the late 1800s. Access to the moat area around the main building for birding is free from October 1 to April 30. The moat can be fair for waterfowl especially in March and April.

24)   American Birding Association, P.O. Box 6599, Colorado Springs, CO 80934; (800)634-7736.

This membership organization publishes *Birding* magazine and a monthly newsletter that contains excellent tips on bird identification and describes good birding locations throughout North America. They also have a sales department which offers members significant discounts on birding books and equipment.

ADDITIONAL READING

Bleed, A. and C. Flowerday, ed. 1989. An atlas of the Sand Hills. Resource Atlas No. 5. Conservation & Survey Div., UNL, Lincoln, NE 68588-0517. 238pp.

Currier, P.J., G.R. Lingle, and J.G. VanDerwalker. 1985. Migratory bird habitat on the Platte and North Platte rivers, Nebraska. Platte River Whooping Crane Maintenance Trust, Grand Island, NE. 177pp. Available for $11 postpaid from Platte River Trust, 2550 N. Diers, Suite H, Grand Island, NE 68803.

Farrar, J., ed. 1985. Birds of Nebraska. Nebraskaland 63(1), Nebr. Game & Parks Comm., Lincoln, NE. 146pp. Out-of-print.

Harrison, G. 1976. Roger Tory Peterson's dozen birding hotspots. Simon & Schuster, New York. 288pp.

Higgins, K. and M. Brashier, eds. 1993. Proc. Missouri River and its tributaries: Piping Plover and Least Tern symposium. South Dakota State Univ., Brookings. Available for $10 from Wildl. & Fisheries Dept., SDSU, Box 2206, Brookings, SD 57007.

Jenkins, A., ed. 1993. The Platte River: an atlas of the Big Bend region. Univ. Nebr- Kearney. 194pp. Available for $23 postpaid from Office of Graduate Studies, UN-K, 1100 Founder's Hall, Kearney, NE 68849.

Johnsgard, P. 1979. Birds of the Great Plains. Univ. Nebr. Press, Lincoln, NE. 539pp.

Johnsgard, P. 1981. Those of the gray wind. Univ. Nebr. Press, Lincoln. 116pp.

Johnsgard, P. 1984. The Platte: Channels in time. Univ. Nebr. Press, Lincoln. 116pp.

Johnsgard, P. 1986. A revised list of the birds of Nebraska and adjacent Plains states. Occ. Papers Nebr. Ornith. Union, No. 6, Lincoln, NE. 170pp. Out-of-print.

Johnsgard, P. 1991. Crane music: a natural history of American cranes. Smithsonian Institution Press, Washington, D.C. 136pp.

Jorde, D. and G. Lingle. 1988. Kleptoparasitism by bald eagles wintering in southcentral Nebraska. J. Field Ornith. 52:183-188.

Lingle, G. R. 1981. Status of American woodcock in Nebraska with notes on a recent breeding record. Prairie Nat. 13:47-51.

Lingle, G. R., and M. A. Hay. 1982. A checklist of the birds of Mormon Island Crane Meadows. Nebr. Bird Rev. 50:27-36.

Lingle, G. R., and T. E. Labedz. 1984. An exceptional "fall" migration of shorebirds along the Big Bend reach of the Platte River. Nebr. Bird Rev. 52:70-71.

Lingle, G. R., and G. L. Krapu. 1986. Winter ecology of bald eagles in south-central Nebraska. Prairie Nat. 18:65-78.

Lingle, G. R. 1987. Status of whooping crane migration habitat within the Great Plains of North America. Pages 331-340 in J.C. Lewis, ed. Proc. 1985 Crane Workshop, Grand Island, NE.

Lingle, G. R. 1989. Winter raptor use of the Platte and North Platte river valleys in south central Nebraska. Prairie Nat. 21:1-16.

Lingle, G. R., and P. A. Bedell. 1989. Nesting ecology of sedge wrens in Hall County, Nebraska. Nebr. Bird Rev. 57:47-49.

Lingle, G. R. 1991. Birder's guide to the Platte River and Rainwater Basin of Nebraska. WildBird 5(3):12-18. (Reprinted in March 1993).

Lingle, G. R., G. A. Wingfield, and J. W. Ziewitz. 1991. The migration ecology of Whooping Cranes in Nebraska, U.S.A. Pages 395-401 in J. Harris, ed. Proc. 1987 International Crane Workshop, Baraboo, WI.

Lingle, G. R. 1992. History and economic impact of crane-watching in central Nebraska. Proc. North American Crane Workshop 6:33-37.

Nebr. Ornith. Union Records Comm. 1988. The official list of the birds of Nebraska. Nebr. Bird Rev 56:86-96.

Pettingill, O. 1953. A guide to bird-finding west of the Mississippi River. Oxford Univ. Press, New York.

Stahlecker, D. and M. Frentzel. 1986. Seasons of the crane. Heritage Assoc., Albuquerque, NM. 55pp.

Stahlecker, D. and R. Urbanek, ed. 1992. Sixth North American Crane Workshop. 179pp. Available from ICF, P.O. Box 447, Baraboo, WI 53913-0447; $20 postpaid.

U. S. Fish & Wildl. Serv. 1981. The Platte River ecology study: special research report. Northern Prairie Wildl. Res. Center, Jamestown, ND. 186pp. Out-of-print.

Whitney, W. and J. Whitney. 1987. Microcosm of the Platte, a guide to Bader Memorial Park Natural Area. Prairie Plains Resource Institute, 1219 16th St., Aurora, NE 68818. 140pp. Available for $10 postpaid.

OTHER TERRESTRIAL VERTEBRATES

As you travel through this area, you will undoubtedly encounter one or more species of terrestrial vertebrates residing here. The following lists contain 10 species of amphibians, 20 species of reptiles, and 53 species of mammals which have been reported in the area. Many of these animals are rare or extremely inconspicuous so your chances of seeing them are slim. You will find that some of these animals have an affinity for roads and are often killed by vehicles. Striped skunk, opossum, raccoon, and white-tailed deer are often seen dead along the highway.

Some are often heard but not seen and these are the toads and frogs. The timing of their chorusing during courtship is as predictable as the arrival of certain species of birds. If you are out watching cranes or waterfowl on a warm day in late March or early April, you will hear western striped chorus frogs, a tiny treefrog about an inch in size with a voice that sounds similar to that produced by running your fingernail along the teeth of a plastic comb. I have heard them as early as March 5 but more commonly around March 21-25. The plains spadefoot toad breeds from early May through August and is stimulated by rainfall. Their call can be confused with a calf bawling. The earliest I've heard them is April 22. The gutteral clucking of southern leopard frogs begins in mid-April while the first trilling of rocky mountain toads is usually in early May. A true sound of summer is the low "jug-o'rum" call of the bullfrog. Late May through July is when this species is heard. Being able to recognize the voices of these "lowly" inhabitants simply adds to the enjoyment of being out in the field on any spring day.

List of Amphibians and Reptiles
(Adapted from Lynch, J. 1985. Annotated checklist of the amphibians and
reptiles of Nebraska. Trans. Nebr. Acad. Sci. 8:33-57)

Salamanders (Order Caudata)   Status

Tiger Salamander   *Ambystoma tigrinum*   Rare

Frogs and Toads (Order Anura)

Northern Cricket Frog	*Acris crepitans*	Rare
Great Plains Toad	*Bufo cognatus*	Common
Rocky Mountain Toad	*Bufo woodhousii*	Abundant
Western Gray Treefrog	*Hyla chrysoscelis*	Rare
W. Striped Chorus Frog	*Pseudacris triseriata*	Abundant
Plains Leopard Frog	*Rana blairi*	Common
Bullfrog	*Rana catesbiana*	Fairly common
Northern Leopard Frog	*Rana pipiens*	Uncommon
Plains Spadefoot Toad	*Spea bombifrons*	Common

Turtles (Order Chelydra)

Snapping Turtle	*Chelydra serpentina*	Common
Painted Turtle	*Chrysemys picta*	Fairly common
Ornate Box Turtle	*Terrapene ornata*	Rare
Spiny Softshell	*Trionyx spiniferus*	Abundant

Lizards (Order Squamata)

Six-lined Racerunner	*Cnemidophorus sexlineatus*	Abundant
Prairie Skink	*Eumeces septentrionalis*	Common
Lesser Earless Lizard	*Holbrookia maculata*	Rare
Northern Prairie Lizard	*Sceloporus undulatus*	Uncommon

Snakes (Order Serpentes)

Blue or Green Racer	*Coluber constrictor*	Rare
Prairie Rattlesnake	*Crotalis viridis*	Rare
Ringneck Snake	*Diadophis punctatus*	Rare
W. Hognose Snake	*Heterodon nasicus*	Rare
Milk Snake	*Lampropeltis triangulum*	Rare
Northern Watersnake	*Nerodia sipedon*	Rare
Smooth Green Snake	*Opheodrys vernalis*	Rare
Bull Snake	*Pituophis catenifer*	Fairly common
Red-bellied Snake	*Storeria occipitomaculata*	Rare
Plains Gartersnake	*Thamnophis radix*	Common
Red-sided Gartersnake	*Thamnophis sirtalis*	Common
Lined Snake	*Tropidoclonian lineatum*	Rare

List of Mammals

(Adapted from Jones, J. and J. Choate. 1980. Annotated list of mammals of
Nebraska. Prairie Nat. 12:43-53)

Order Marsupialia		Status
Virginia Opossum	*Didelphis virginiana*	Common

Order Insectivora

Masked Shrew	*Sorex cinereus*	Common
N. Short-tailed Shrew	*Blarina brevicauda*	Common
Least Shrew	*Cryptotis parva*	Uncommon
Eastern Mole	*Scalopus aquaticus*	Fairly common

Order Chiroptera

Big Brown Bat	*Eptesicus fuscus*	Common
Red Bat	*Lasiurus borealis*	Common
Hoary Bat	*Lasiurus cinereus*	Uncommon
Brazilian Free-tailed Bat	*Tadarida brasiliensis*	Rare

Order Lagomorpha

Eastern Cottontail	*Sylvilagus floridanus*	Abundant
Black-tailed Jackrabbit	*Lepus californicus*	Common
White-tailed Jackrabbit	*Lepus townsendii*	Rare

Order Rodentia

Woodchuck	*Marmota monax*	Rare
Franklin's Ground Squirrel	*Spermophilus franklinii*	Uncommon
Thirteen-lined Ground Squirrel	*Spermophilus tridecemlineatus*	Abundant
Black-tailed Prairie Dog	*Cynomys ludovicianus*	Uncommon
Fox Squirrel	*Sciurus niger*	Abundant
Plains Pocket Gopher	*Geomys bursarius*	Common
Plains Pocket Mouse	*Perognathus flavescens*	Uncommon
Hispid Pocket Mouse	*Perognathus hispidus*	Uncommon
Ord's Kangaroo Rat	*Dipodomys ordii*	Uncommon
Beaver	*Castor canadensis*	Abundant
W. Harvest Mouse	*Reithrodontomys megalotis*	Common
Plains Harvest Mouse	*Reithrodontomys montanus*	Uncommon
White-footed Mouse	*Peromyscus leucopus*	Abundant
Deer Mouse	*Peromyscus maniculatus*	Abundant
N. Grasshopper Mouse	*Onychomys leucogaster*	Fairly common
Hispid Cotton Rat	*Sigmodon hispidus*	Rare
Eastern Woodrat	*Neotoma floridana*	Rare

Prairie Vole	*Microtus ochrogaster*	Abundant
Meadow Vole	*Microtus pennsylvanicus*	Abundant
Muskrat	*Ondatra ziebethicus*	Abundant
Southern Bog Lemming	*Synaptomys cooperi*	Rare
House Mouse	*Mus musculus*	Abundant
Norway Rat	*Rattus norvegicus*	Common
Meadow Jumping Mouse	*Zapus hudsonius*	Uncommon
Porcupine	*Erethizon dorsatum*	Rare

Order Carnivora

Coyote	*Canis latrans*	Abundant
Red Fox	*Vulpes vulpes*	Fairly common
Raccoon	*Procyon lotor*	Abundant
Long-tailed Weasel	*Mustela frenata*	Uncommon
Least Weasel	*Mustela nivalis*	Uncommon
Mink	*Mustela vison*	Common
Badger	*Taxidea taxus*	Fairly common
Striped Skunk	*Mephitis mephitis*	Abundant
River Otter	*Lutra canadensis*	Reintroduced
Bobcat	*Felix rufus*	Rare

Order Artiodactyla

Wapiti	*Cervus elaphus*	Accidental
Mule Deer	*Odocoileus hemionus*	Common
White-tailed Deer	*Odocoileus virginianus*	Abundant
Moose	*Alces alces*	Accidental
Bison	*Bison bison*	Extirpated

SIGHTING REPORT FORM

This form is intended as a convenience for documenting unusual sightings. Attach additional sheets as necessary.

1. SPECIES _____
2. NUMBER SEEN & AGE (eg. 2 adults & 3 imm.) _____
3. DESCRIPTION (plumage; color of eyes, beak, legs; wing bars; eye stripe or ring; size) _____

_____

_____

_____

_____

_____

4. VOICE (song given in flight, perched, etc.) _____

_____

5. BEHAVIOR _____

_____

6. HABITAT _____
7. EXACT LOCATION OF SIGHTING _____
8. DATE & TIME _____
9. DURATION OF SIGHTING _____
10. DISTANCE FROM BIRD & OPTICS USED _____

_____

11. HOW WAS IT DISTINGUISHED FROM SIMILAR SPECIES?

_____

12. PHOTOGRAPHED? _____ BY WHOM? _____
13. FIELD GUIDES USED _____
14. HOW FAMILIAR ARE YOU WITH SPECIES? _____

_____

15. YOUR NAME & ADDRESS _____

_____

Thank-you for submitting this report. Please return this form to:

Records Committee
Nebraska Ornithologists' Union
W-436 Nebraska Hall
University of Nebraska- Lincoln
Lincoln, NE 68588-0514

A

American Birding Association, 106
American Ornithologist's Union, 85, 98
Amphibians, 110, 111
Audubon River Conference, 104
Audubon Society Chapters
  Big Bend, 105
  Grand Island Chapter, 105
Aurora, 41, 101, 102, 109
Avocet, American, 23, 31, 52, 91
Ayr Lake, 23

B

Bader Memorial Park, 41, 69, 70, 75, 101, 109
Bassway Strip State Wildlife Area, 27
Beaver, 28, 42, 112
Big Bend, 13, 53, 57, 105, 107, 108
Biogeography, 12
Birding, 106
Bison, 9, 111, 113
Bittern
  American, 88
  Least, 88
Blackbird
  Brewer's, 98
  Red-winged, 97
  Rusty, 98
  Yellow-headed, 41, 49, 85, 98
Blind, 27, 35, 45, 52, 53, 67, 100, 101, 102, 103
Blue Hole State Wildlife Area, 28
Bluebird
  Eastern, 35, 36, 49, 78, 79, 94
  Mountain, 94
Bobolink, 27, 35, 36, 80, 82, 83, 97
Bobwhite, Northern, 90
Braided River, 100
Brant, 88
Breeding Bird Survey, 71, 76
Bufflehead, 89
Bunting
  Indigo, 12, 23, 45, 97
  Lark, 97
  Lazuli, 12, 96
  Painted, 97

C

Canvasback, 54, 89
Cardinal, Northern, 96
Catbird, Gray, 95
Cather, Willa, 83
Central Community College, 85
Central Nebraska Public Power and Irrigation District, 57, 103
Chat, Yellow-breasted, 96
Cheyenne Bottoms, 62, 67
Chickadee, Black-capped, 94
Cholera, 16, 23, 58
Christmas Bird Count, 86, 105
Chukar, 37
Columbus, 104
Coot, American, 90
Cormorant, Double-crested, 49, 88
Cornhusker State Wildlife Area, 36
Cottonmill City Park, 27
Cottonwood, 16, 23, 28, 36, 56, 62, 72, 73
County
  Gosper, 49
  Lincoln, 53
  Merrick, 41, 70
Cowbird, Brown-headed, 82, 98
Coyote, 70
Crane, 11, 36, 104, 110
  Sandhill, 11, 27, 35, 36, 51, 52, 53, 54, 70, 84, 90, 101, 102
  Whooping, 24, 45, 49, 50, 53, 58, 59, 61, 90, 104, 105, 107, 108
Crane Meadows Nature Center, 35, 36, 69, 78, 82, 102
Crane Watch, 104
Creeper, Brown, 94
Critical Habitat, Whooping Crane, 59
Crossbill
  Red, 98
  White-winged, 98
Crow, American, 94
Cuckoo
  Black-billed, 92
  Yellow-billed, 92

Curlew
  Eskimo, 9, 61, 91
  Long-billed, 91

D

Dannebrog, 68
Deep Well State Wildlife Area, 41, 85
Deer
  Mule, 31
  White-tailed, 42, 110
Dickcissel, 27, 35, 80, 97
Dove
  Inca, 92
  Mourning, 92
  Rock, 92
Dowitcher
  Long-billed, 92
  Short-billed, 92
Duck
  American Black, 89
  Ring-necked, 54, 89
  Ruddy, 54, 89
  Wood, 55, 70, 88
Dunlin, 91

E

Eagle
  Bald, 27, 28, 32, 36, 49, 56, 57, 62,
  64, 70, 89, 103, 108
  Golden, 31, 64, 90
Egret
  Cattle, 62, 88
  Great, 62, 88
  Snowy, 62, 88

F

Falcon
  Peregrine, 50, 58, 90
  Prairie, 31, 62, 64, 90
Finch
  House, 86, 98
  Purple, 98
Flicker
  Northern, 73, 93
  Red-shafted, 12, 73
  Yellow-shafted, 12, 73

Flycatcher
  Great Crested, 93
  Least, 93
  Olive-sided, 93
  Willow, 27, 37, 75, 93
  Yellow-bellied, 93
Forbs, 83
Fort Kearny, 45, 53, 101

G

Gadwall, 54, 89
Geese, 16, 23, 27, 31, 37, 41, 45, 49,
54, 55, 58
Gibbon, 27, 100
Godwit
  Hudsonian, 91
  Marbled, 41, 91
Golden-Plover, American, 23, 90
Goldeneye, Common, 89
Goldfinch, American, 37, 98
Goose
  Canada, 27, 45, 54, 55, 56, 88
  Snow, 31, 41, 54, 55, 88
  Greater White-fronted, 45, 54, 88
  Ross', 31, 37, 54, 55, 88
Goshawk, Northern, 64, 90
Grackle
  Common, 98
  Great-tailed, 49, 85, 98
Grand Island, 13, 14, 35, 51, 61, 67, 70,
72, 85, 86, 100, 105, 106, 107, 108
Grebe
  Eared, 49, 88
  Horned, 88
  Pied-billed, 37, 88
  Western, 88
Grosbeak
  Black-headed, 12, 96
  Blue, 37, 49, 96
  Evening, 98
  Pine, 98
  Rose-breasted, 12, 23, 27, 35, 37, 96
Grouse, 102
  Sharp-tailed, 37, 67, 68, 90, 103
Grus Americana, 105

Gull
  Bonaparte's, 71, 92
  Franklin's, 71, 92
  Herring, 92
  Ring-billed, 71, 92

H

Hall County Park, 37
Harrier, Northern, 31, 32, 36, 62, 89
Harvard Marsh *See Waterfowl Production Area*
Hastings, 23, 61, 72, 85, 104
  Cemetery, 23
  Museum, 61, 104
Hawk
  Broad-winged, 90
  Cooper's, 90
  Ferruginous, 27, 62, 90
  Red-tailed, 62, 66, 90
  Rough-legged, 36, 62, 64, 90
  Sharp-shinned, 90
  Swainson's, 62, 64, 90
Heron
  Great Blue, 24, 49, 62, 88
  Green, 62, 88
  Little Blue, 62, 88
Hershey, 53, 103
Hike Bike Trail, 45, 75, 101
Hiking, 31, 32, 36, 37, 41
Historical Marker, 23
Holdrege, 103
Hummingbird
  Broad-tailed, 93
  Ruby-throated, 93
  Rufous, 93

I

Ibis, White-faced, 45, 88
ICF Bugle, 106
Imax Theater, 104
International Crane Foundation, 106

J

Jay, Blue, 94
Jeffrey's Island, 49
Junco, Dark-eyed, 82, 97

K

Kearney, 11, 45, 51, 53, 56, 59, 61, 67, 70, 73, 75, 101, 104, 105, 107
Kenesaw Lagoon, 24
Kestrel, American, 90
Killdeer, 66, 91
Kingbird
  Eastern, 75, 93
  Western, 75, 93
Kingfisher, Belted, 93
Kinglet
  Golden-crowned, 94
  Ruby-crowned, 94
Kite
  Mississippi, 12, 66, 89
  White-tailed, 89
Knot, Red, 91
Kuralt, Charles, 68

L

Lark, Horned, 32, 94
Latin America, 87
Leopold, Aldo, 69
Lexington, 13, 57, 59
Lincoln, 104
Little Blue River, 23
Longspur, Lapland, 97
Loon, Common, 28, 88

M

Magpie, Black-billed, 36, 76, 94
Mallard, 27, 54, 55, 56, 64, 89
Mammals, 110, 112
Martin, Purple, 94
McConaughy, Lake, 57, 103
Meadowlark
  Eastern, 84, 97
  Western, 83, 84, 98
Merganser
  Common, 54, 89
  Hooded, 89
  Red-breasted, 89
Merlin, 90
Mockingbird, Northern, 12, 37, 95

Mormon Island Crane Meadows (MICM), 35, 61, 64, 68, 75, 76, 78, 81, 82, 108
Mormons, 71

N

National Audubon Society, 27, 100, 105
Nebraska Bird Hotline, 100
Nebraska Bird Review, 87, 104
Nebraska Game & Parks Commission, 11, 53, 102
Nebraska Ornithologists' Union, 72, 87, 104
Nebraska Public Power District, 28, 61, 104
Neotropical Migrant, 87, 98
Night-Heron
  Black-crowned, 45, 49, 88
  Yellow-crowned, 88
Nighthawk, Common, 93
Nine-Mile Bridge, 36
North America, 5, 12, 59, 87, 106, 108
North American Crane Working Group, 106
North Dakota, 85
North Platte, 85, 102, 103
North Platte Field Office, 53, 102
North Platte River, 53, 73, 100, 107, 108
Nutcracker, Clark's, 94
Nuthatch
  Red-breasted, 94
  White-breasted, 94

O

Observability Code, 87, 98
Ogallala Aquifer, 12
Omaha, 58, 102
Oregon Trail, 23
Oriole
  Baltimore, 12, 85
  Bullock's, 12, 85
  Northern, 85, 98
  Orchard, 98
Osprey, 89
Otter, River, 37
Ovenbird, 96

Owl
  Barn, 92
  Barred, 93
  Burrowing, 72, 92
  Great Horned, 62, 64, 92
  Long-eared, 37, 50, 93
  Northern Saw-whet, 93
  Short-eared, 31, 32, 36, 64, 93
  Snowy, 92

P

Passerines, 24, 36
Pelican, American White, 41, 49, 88
Phalarope
  Red, 92
  Red-necked, 92
  Wilson's, 92
Pheasant, Ring-necked, 90
Phillips Basin, 41
Phoebe
  Eastern, 93
  Say's, 93
Pigeon, Passenger, 9
Pintail, Northern, 54, 55, 89
Pintail State Wildlife Area, 41, 55
Pipit
  American, 95
  Sprague's, 95
Platte River, 12, 13, 16, 11, 19, 27, 28, 35, 41, 45, 49, 51, 53, 54, 56, 57, 58, 59, 60, 61, 67, 69, 73, 76, 82, 100, 101, 102, 103, 105, 107, 108
Platte River Journal, 105
Platte River Road, 49, 53
Platte River Whooping Crane Maintenance Trust, 35, 61, 100, 102, 107
Plover
  Black-bellied, 90
  Mountain, 91
  Piping, 5, 16, 27, 28, 36, 49, 60, 91, 104, 107
  Semipalmated, 41, 66, 91
  Snowy, 91
Poison Ivy, 12
Poorwill, Common, 93

Prairie-Chicken, Greater, 35, 37, 67, 90, 103
Prairie Dog, 31, 45, 72, 73, 112
Prairie Plains Resource Institute, 41, 101, 109
Pronghorn, 9

R

Rail
    Black, 90
    King, 41, 90
    Virginia, 49, 90
    Yellow, 90
Rainwater Basin, 12, 13, 16, 11, 19, 31, 41, 54, 55, 57, 58, 59, 62, 64, 67, 101, 102, 108
Rainwater Basin Wetland District, 101
Rattlesnake, 12
Records Committee, 87, 114
Redhead, 54, 89
Redpoll, Common, 98
Redstart, American, 96
Regal Fritillaries, 42
Reptiles, 110, 111
Robin, American, 95
Rosy-finch, Gray-crowned, 98
Rowe Sanctuary, 27, 69, 75, 78, 100

S

Sanderling, 66, 91
Sandhills, 37, 67, 80, 82
Sandpiper,
    Baird's, 66, 91
    Buff-breasted, 66, 92
    Least, 66, 91
    Pectoral, 45, 66, 91
    Semipalmated, 91
    Solitary, 91
    Spotted, 91
    Stilt, 49, 92
    Upland, 27, 35, 36, 68, 80, 82, 83, 91
    Western, 49, 91
    White-rumped, 66, 91
Sapsucker, Yellow-bellied, 93
Scaup
    Greater, 89
    Lesser, 54, 89

Scoter
    Surf, 89
    White-winged, 89
Screech-Owl, Eastern, 66, 92
Shoemaker Island, 35, 36, 70, 78
Shorebirds, 23, 24, 41, 45, 49, 50, 58, 61, 62, 66, 67, 108
Shoveler, Northern, 54, 89
Shrike
    Loggerhead, 80, 95
    Northern, 12, 36, 95
Sighting Report Form, 87, 114
Siskin, Pine, 12, 98
Snipe, Common, 92
Solitaire, Townsend's, 95
Sora, 49, 90
South America, 68, 80
Sparrow, 23, 31, 36
    American Tree, 31, 36, 37, 82, 97
    Chipping, 37, 97
    Clay-colored, 37, 97
    Field, 97
    Fox, 97
    Grasshopper, 35, 81, 97
    Harris', 31, 82, 97
    Henslow's, 97
    House, 78, 98
    Lark, 97
    Le Conte's, 97
    Lincoln's, 97
    Savannah, 97
    Sharp-tailed, 97
    Song, 97
    Swamp, 97
    Vesper, 97
    White-crowned, 82, 97
    White-throated, 97
Starling, European, 73, 95
State Bird, 84
Stilt, Black-necked, 91
Stuhr Museum, 106
Summer Orientation About Rivers (SOAR), 101
Swallow
    Bank, 94
    Barn, 94
    Cliff, 76, 94
    Rough-winged, 94

Tree, 94
Violet-green, 94
Swan
Mute, 88
Trumpeter, 88
Tundra, 88
Swift, Chimney, 93

T

Tanager
Scarlet, 96
Summer, 96
Taylor Ranch, 37, 67, 69, 82
Teal
Blue-winged, 54, 56, 89
Cinnamon, 31, 37, 49, 54, 89
Green-winged, 54, 89
Tern
Black, 41, 92
Caspian, 92
Common, 92
Forster's, 49, 92
Least, 16, 27, 28, 36, 49, 60, 92, 104, 107
The Nature Conservancy, 102
Thirty-Two Mile Creek Watershed, 23
Thrasher, Brown, 95
Thrush, 37
Gray-cheeked, 95
Hermit, 95
Swainson's, 95
Tick, 11
Lone Star, 12
Wood, 12
Titmouse, Tufted, 94
Tornado, 14, 16
Tours, 51, 53, 100, 101, 102, 104, 105
Towhee, Rufous-sided, 36, 97
Trail
Bluebird, 78, 105
Mark Bolin Nature, 100
Tropic of Cancer, 87, 98
Turkey, Wild, 36, 90
Turnstone, Ruddy, 91

U

U.S. Ammunitions Depot, 31, 85

U.S. Fish & Wildlife Service, 41, 101, 102, 105
Unison Call, 106
University of Nebraska State Museum, 61

V

Veery, 95
Vireo, 23
Bell's, 27, 28, 45, 95
Philadelphia, 95
Red-eyed, 95
Solitary, 95
Warbling, 42, 95
Yellow-throated, 95
Vulture, Turkey, 89

W

Waders, 24, 32, 41, 45, 49, 62
Wapiti, 9, 113
Warbler, 23, 37
Bay-breasted, 96
Black-and-white, 96
Black-throated Blue, 96
Black-throated Green, 96
Blackburnian, 96
Blackpoll, 96
Blue-winged, 95
Cape May, 96
Chestnut-sided, 96
Golden-winged, 95
Kentucky, 96
Magnolia, 96
Mourning, 96
Nashville, 95
Orange-crowned, 95
Palm, 96
Tennessee, 95
Wilson's, 96
Yellow, 41, 95
Yellow-rumped, 41, 96
Yellow-throated, 96
Waterfowl, 16, 11, 23, 24, 27, 31, 32, 41, 50, 54, 55, 56, 58, 101, 106, 110

Waterfowl Production Area (WPA)
   Funk Lagoon, 49, 55, 59, 85
   Gleason, 45, 55, 59
   Harvard Marsh, 31, 55
   Johnson, 49, 59
   Massie, 55
   Prairie Dog, 45, 59
   Springer, 41
Waterthrush
   Lousiana, 96
   Northern, 96
Waxwing
   Bohemian, 95
   Cedar, 42, 95
Welsch, Roger, 68
Whimbrel, 91
Whooping Crane, 5
Whooping Crane Conservation
Association, 105
Widow, Chuck-will's, 93
Wigeon
   American, 54, 89
   Eurasian, 89
Wildflowers, 37
Willet, 41, 91
Wings Over the Platte, 105
Wood-Pewee, Eastern, 35, 93
Woodcock, American, 35, 69, 92, 108
Woodpecker
   Downy, 93
   Hairy, 93
   Red-bellied, 93
   Red-headed, 73, 74, 93
Wren
   Bewick's, 94
   Carolina, 94
   House, 78, 94
   Marsh, 94
   Rock, 94
   Sedge, 35, 76, 77, 78, 94
   Winter, 94

Y

Yellowlegs
   Greater, 66, 91
   Lesser, 66, 91
Yellowthroat, Common, 41, 96

Order Form

BIRDING CRANE RIVER: NEBRASKA'S PLATTE
by Gary R. Lingle

HARRIER PUBLISHING
P.O. Box 5352
Grand Island, NE 68802-5352

Name_____ Date_____

Address_____

City_____State/Prov_____ Zip_____

	Amt. Enclosed
# of Copies _____ X **$11.95** each =	_____
Nebraska residents add sales tax	_____
Postage & Handling	_____
TOTAL	_____

Postage and Handling: $3.00 for the first book; $1.00 thereafter. Foreign orders add an additional $1.00 per book.

Cash with Order; please make checks payable to **Harrier Publishing**.